TWELVE STRIKING SERMONS

TWELVE
STRIKING
SERMONS

C. H. Spurgeon

BAKER BOOK HOUSE
Grand Rapids, Michigan

Reprinted by Baker Book House

First printing, November 1971
Second printing, May 1973
Third printing, December 1974
Fourth printing, June 1976
Fifth printing, February 1978
Sixth printing, February 1980

ISBN: 0-8010-7941-1

PHOTOLITHOPRINTED BY CUSHING - MALLOY, INC.
ANN ARBOR, MICHIGAN, UNITED STATES OF AMERICA
1 9 8 0

CONTENTS

TWELVE STRIKING SERMONS

THE MINSTREL

A SERMON

THE text is a somewhat singular one, but I hope it will suggest a profitable idea.

"But now bring me a minstrel. And it came to pass, when the minstrel played, that the hand of the Lord came upon him."— 2 Kings iii. 15.

Elisha needed that the Holy Spirit should come upon him to inspire him with prophetic utterances. "Holy men of God spake as they were moved by the Holy Ghost." We need that the hand of the Lord should be laid upon us, for we can never open our mouths in wisdom except we are under the divine touch. Now, the Spirit of God works according to His own will. "The wind bloweth where it listeth," and the Spirit of God operates as He chooseth. Elisha could not prophesy just when he liked; he must wait until the Spirit of God came upon him, and the Spirit of God could come or not even as He pleased. Elisha had noticed that the Spirit of God acted upon him most freely when his mind was restful and subdued. He found himself best prepared for the heavenly voice when the noise within his soul was hushed, and every disturbing emotion was quieted. Having ascertained this fact by observation he acted upon it. He could not create the wind of the Spirit, but he could set his sail to receive it, and he did so.

At the particular time alluded to in the text Elisha had been greatly irritated by the sight of Jehoram, the king of Israel, the son of Ahab and Jezebel. In the true spirit of his old master, Elijah, the prophet let Jehoram know what he thought of him; and having delivered his soul, he very naturally felt agitated and distressed, and unfit to be the mouthpiece for the Spirit of God. He knew that the hand of the Lord would not rest upon him while he was in that state, and therefore he said, "Bring me a minstrel." The original Hebrew conveys the idea of a man accustomed to play upon the harp. Listening to the dulcet tones which were produced by a skilful harper, who very likely sang one of David's psalms to the music, the prophet waited awhile, and then the hand of the Lord came upon him. Under the influence of minstrelsy his mind grew quiet, his agitation subsided, his thoughts were collected, and the Spirit of God spake through him. It was a most commendable thing for him to use the means which he had found at other times helpful, though still his sole reliance was upon the hand of the Lord. It would seem from a passage in the First Book of Samuel that Elisha was not the only prophet who had found music helpful, for we read, "Thou shalt meet a company of prophets coming down from the high place with a psaltery, and a tabret, and a pipe, and a harp, before them; and they shall prophesy." Elisha, like his predecessors, only used a natural means for putting himself into readiness for receiving supernatural help.

Let us see if we can bring forth the practical lesson which this incident may teach us.

I. First: here is a lesson to those who wish to serve God, and to speak in His name. LET US STRIVE TO BE IN A FIT STATE FOR THE LORD'S WORK. If we know of anything that will put our mind into such a condition that the Spirit of God is likely to work upon us and speak through us, let us make use of it. Elisha cried, "Bring me a minstrel"; let us also say—bring me that which will be helpful to me. The harper could be of no service to Elisha for bringing him inspiration; but by putting him into a calm, equable state of mind he prepared him for the heavenly communication, and removed from his soul that which would have hindered the divine working.

It is very evident that we, too, like the prophet, have *our hindrances*. We are at times unfit for the Master's use. Our minds are disarranged, the machinery is out of order, the sail is furled, the pipe is blocked up, the whole soul is out of gear. The hindrance in Elisha's case came from *his surroundings*. He was in a camp; a camp where three nations mixed their discordant voices; a noisy, ill-disciplined camp, and a camp ready to perish for thirst. There was no water, and the men-at-arms were perishing; the confusion and clamour must have been great. Prophetic thought could scarcely command itself amid the uproar, the discontent, the threatening from thousands of thirsty men. Three kings had waited on the prophet; but this would not have disconcerted him had not one of them been Jehoram, the son of Ahab, and Jezebel. What memories were awakened in the mind of Elijah's servant by the sight of the man in whom the proud dame of Sidon and her base-minded consort lived again. Naboth's vineyard must have come to his mind, and the stern threat of Elijah—"The dogs shall eat Jezebel by the wall of Jezreel." "For there was none like unto Ahab, which did sell himself to work wickedness in the sight of the Lord, whom Jezebel his wife stirred up."

Elisha acted rightly, and bravely. When he saw Jehoram coming to him for help, he challenged him thus—"What have I to do with thee? Get thee to the prophets of thy father, and to the prophets of thy mother." When the king humbly and with bated breath confessed that he saw the hand of Jehovah in bringing the three kings together, the prophet scarcely moderated his tone, but exclaimed, "As the Lord of hosts liveth, before whom I stand, surely, were it not that I regard the presence of Jehoshaphat, the king of Judah, I would not look toward thee, nor see thee." It was fit that he should be in that temper; the occasion demanded it. Still it was not a fit preface to the inward whisper of the Spirit of God, and the prophet did not feel ready for his work: the circumstances were not soothing or elevating, and so he said, "Bring me a minstrel."

Do you not occasionally find yourself in an unhappy position? You have to preach, or to teach a class in school, or to carry an edifying word to a sick person; but everything distracts you. What with noise, or domestic trouble, or sinful neighbours, or the railing words of some wicked man, you cannot get into a fit frame of mind. You have had a duty to do which has caused you much pain and disquietude, and you cannot get over it, for everything conspires to worry you. Little things grieve great minds. The very sight of some individuals will throw a preacher off the rails. I know that the height of the pulpit, the thinness of the audience, the sleepiness of a hearer, or the heaviness of the atmosphere, may put the preacher's heart out of tune, and incapacitate him for the blessing. Yes, we have our hindrances even as Elisha had.

Elisha's hindrances lay mainly in *his inward feelings*: he could not feel the hand of the Lord upon him until the inner warfare had been pacified. The prophet's spirits were depressed. He saw before him the king of Edom, an idolater; the king of Israel, a votary of the calves of Jeroboam; and Jehoshaphat, the man of God, in confederacy with them. This last must have pained him as much as anything. What hope was there for the cause of truth and holiness when even a godly prince was in alliance with Jezebel's son? This burdened the heart of the man of God. Everything was wrong, and going worse and worse. The warnings of Elijah and his own teachings seemed to go for nothing; the honour of God was forgotten, and the cause of evil triumphed.

Moreover, the servant of God must have been the subject of a fierce internal conflict between two sets of thoughts. Indignation and pity strove within his heart. His justice and his piety made him feel that he could have nothing to do with two idolatrous kings; but pity and humanity made him wish to

deliver the army from perishing by thirst. Like a patriot, he
sympathized with his people; but, like a prophet, he was jealous
for his God. The men of Judah and Israel, whatever they might
be in character, were the Lord's people by covenant; he could
not let them die: yet they had broken that covenant, and how
could he help them? The prophet was perplexed, and his heart
grew heavy. How can we do the Lord's work when we are
cast down in spirit? The joy of the Lord is our strength, and
when we lose it our hands are feeble. When the heart is torn
with inner conflict how can we speak words of comfort to those
who are weary? We have need to escape from this inward
strife before we can become sons of consolation to others. While
rent with conflicting feeling, there was no rest in the prophet's
spirit; and the hand of the Lord did not come upon him. Most
wisely he did not attempt to speak in the name of the Lord,
but sought for a means by which his excitement could be
allayed.

In the face of many hindrances we shall be wise if we imitate
him. When we feel ourselves cumbered with much serving we
shall act discreetly if we pause in it, and take Mary's place, for
awhile, at least, and sit at Jesus' feet; or, if the service must
be done at once, it will be well to use the readiest means for
preparing the mind for doing it. If I go to do the Lord's work
with a vexed or distracted mind, I shall do it badly. Perhaps
I shall do more harm than good. I shall spill the cup of consolation if I am all in a tremble myself. God's servants should
serve their Master well: the best we can render falls short of
His deservings; but it would be a pity to do less than our very
best. The prophet said, "Bring me a minstrel. And it came
to pass, when the minstrel played, that the hand of the Lord
came upon him."

But what are our *helps* when we are pressed with hindrances?
Is there anything which in our case may be as useful as a
harp? "Bring me a minstrel," said the prophet, for his mind
was easily moved by that charming art. Music and song soothed
and calmed, and cheered him.

> "Through every pulse the music stole,
> And held high converse with his soul."

On the wings of melody his mind rose above the noisy camp,
and floated far away from the loathed presence of Jehoram; the
melting mystic strain laid all his passions asleep, and his soul
was left in silence to hear the voice of the Lord. Well did Luther
say, "Music is the art of the prophets, the only art that can
calm the agitations of the soul; it is one of the most magnificent
and delightful presents God has given us."

Among our own helps *singing* holds a chief place; as saith the apostle, "Speaking to yourselves in psalms and hymns and spiritual songs, singing and making melody in your heart to the Lord." Note how he connects it with peace in his epistle to the Colossians: "Let the peace of God rule in your hearts . . . teaching and admonishing one another in psalms and hymns and spiritual songs, singing with grace in your hearts to the Lord." "I cannot sing," says one. You need not sing as sweetly as Asaph and Heman, and other sweet birds of paradise whose names we read in Scripture; but we should all sing better if we sang more. Those with cracked voices would be kind if they would not sing quite so loudly in the congregation, for they grievously disturb other people; but they might get alone and have good times with themselves, where nobody could complain of their strong voices and lusty tones. It is good to sing praises unto the Lord, and a part of its goodness lies in the comfort which it brings. It is not without significance, that after supper, before our Lord went to His great sacrifice, He sang a hymn.

Suppose, however, that singing has no such power over you; let me recommend to you the quiet *reading* of a chapter of God's Word. Go upstairs and open the Book, and think upon a few verses. If you are much perplexed, read that blessed chapter which begins, "Let not your heart be troubled: ye believe in God, believe also in me." Those verses act like a charm upon many minds: many and many a time a storm has subsided into a calm by the reading of those words. Some such passage read quietly will often operate as the harper acted upon Elisha. If time be pressing, see what is the text for the day in the almanack; or choose out some one precious promise which in other days was sweet to you. It is wonderful the effect of a single verse of Scripture when the Spirit of God applies it to the soul. There is music to a miser in the jingling of his money bag: but what music can equal this—"All things work together for good to them that love God, to them who are the called according to his purpose"? If you are in poverty, what melody lies in this: "Trust in the Lord, and do good; so shalt thou dwell in the land, and verily thou shalt be fed." What power would come upon the soul to calm and quiet it, and make it ready for the hand of God, if we would grasp a single line of Scripture and suck the honey out of it till our soul is filled with sweetness.

You will find it equal to bringing a minstrel, and perhaps even more efficient, if you will get alone to *pray*. That horrible Rabshakeh's letter—you read it, and then you wished you had never seen it. You put it behind the glass, but you fetch it out again, and read it again, and cry, "What a trial is this! who can bear it?" There is a kind of basilisk power in an abominable letter, so that you feel compelled to read it again and again. Can you not break the spell? What is the wisest course? Go upstairs, open it wide, spread it before the Lord, and say, "O Lord, thou hast seen letters like this before; for thy servant Hezekiah showed thee one." I would say of every sorrow, "Pray over it."

An old divine, after he had heard a young minister preach a poor discourse, said to him, "Sir, I beg you to try and pray that sermon over." He replied that he could not pray it over. Now, a sermon that cannot be prayed over ought never to be preached at all, and a trouble that you cannot pray over is a trouble which you ought not to have. It must be a grief of your own making; it cannot be a trial of God's sending. Tell the Lord your affliction, and the bitterness of it will be past, and you will go back to your daily service calm and quiet, fitted for the hand of the Lord to be laid upon you.

It may be you will find fittest help in *Christian association.* I commend this to those believers who are seldom fit for God to use because they are morose and fault-finding. You ought to say, "Bring me a minstrel—find me some praying sister whom I may talk with, or find me some genial brother who rejoices in the Lord, and let me converse with such." It may be that the Master will join you and make a third, and then shall your heart be glad. Much misery is caused by Christians attempting to go to heaven alone. You remember how Mr. Bunyan describes Christian as journeying alone at first; he soon picked up with Hopeful, and then he was more cheery. As for Christiana and Mercy, and the family, they scarcely could have gone on pilgrimage at all if it had not been for Mr. Greatheart: but when they all went in company, with Mr. Greatheart to lead the band, they could sing all the way to the gates of the Celestial City. Holy converse acts as a minstrel to the Spirit.

II. My second word is to those who have not yet found the Lord. WE SHOULD USE EVERY MEANS TO OBTAIN THE TOUCH OF THE DIVINE HAND. There are some here present who do not yet know whether they are believers in Christ or not: and I am sure I cannot tell them. I hope they are believers, for they are sincerely desirous of eternal salvation, but sometimes I am afraid they are not, for they do not appear to understand the meaning of the finished work of Christ. What are those, who are earnestly seeking the Lord, to do? There is but one answer, "Believe in the Lord Jesus Christ, and thou shalt be saved." Faith is the one and only course commanded. But some one replied, "Alas, I cannot get at that." But, my friend, you must get at it, or perish. Without faith it is impossible to please God.

Still, to help you, let me urge you to do this which lies near at hand: if you cannot feel that the Spirit of God will bless you as you are, call for some minstrel, who may aid you in your search after the blessing. If there be any subordinate means which may be helpful, use it with a view to the higher and better thing. I would first say—If you feel that you have not the faith which you ought to have, *use what faith you have*. It is wonderful what an immense amount of possibility lies in a mustard seed of faith. It is a very small, tiny thing; but sow it, and it will grow. You have not enough faith to believe that Christ *will* save you, but you have enough to feel sure that Christ *can* save you. That is something: hold on to it and follow it out to its fair conclusions. If a man has not money enough to pay for a week's provisions, let him not starve; but let him spend what he has, hoping that more will come. Have you a small dust of faith? use that, and it will multiply.

If you want to feel the hand of the Lord, I would next say, Go and *hear a sound, earnest, lively preacher*. I am advising you to do as I acted myself. I was muddled, and could not exercise faith, and so I resolved to obey that other precept, "Hear, and your soul shall live."

If you long for faith, listen to the preacher who preaches the gospel most simply and most forcibly. Perhaps you say, "I have been listening to a very clever minister, a very intellectual minister, and his word has never been blessed to my soul." Then shift your place, and say, "Bring me a minstrel"; for then it may be that the hand of the Lord may be upon you. It is better to go a hundred miles to hear a faithful minister than to listen to a man from whom you get no good because he happens to preach near you. Men go many miles to a skilful physician, or a healing fountain. When we are in earnest to find Christ we shall have the sense to go where He is most honoured and most spoken of.

"But suppose I have attended such a ministry, and have found no good; what shall I do?" Why, the Scripture says, "Believe in the Lord Jesus Christ, and thou shalt be saved." Still, if you cannot get at this for the moment, *attend earnest meetings* where souls have been converted, and many have been brought to Jesus' feet. Trust not to preachers or meetings; but, still, go where the rain is falling, and there may be a drop for you. If a ministry is blessing others, resort to it, praying, "O Lord, *bless* me." Our immediate need is the hand of the Lord, and we may be made ready to receive it by hearing the gospel; therefore let us diligently incline our ear to the heavenly word.

Let me also advise you to *read gracious books*. Ask Christian people what writings were blessed to their conversion, and carefully study the same. There is no book for saving souls like the Bible. Say, "Bring me a minstrel," and read the Scriptures again and again. The Lord Jesus feedeth among the lilies: get among the beds of lilies, and you will find Him there. Oh, how many have found Christ when they have been searching the Scriptures to see "whether those things were so."

I would also strongly recommend you to *get a good deal alone*. You poor souls, who cannot find Christ, and do not seem to understand what it is to believe in Him, should think much, and meditate much, upon Jesus and His cross. David said, "I thought on my ways, and turned my feet into thy testimonies." If you want a minstrel, think of your sin, your sin against your God, till it breaks your heart; then think of Christ, His nature, His work, His love, His deeds of mercy: think of the Holy Spirit, and His power to renew, regenerate, comfort, sanctify: think over those precious truths of the word of God, which are set there on purpose to be beacons to light souls to Christ, and while you are thinking of these it shall be to you as when the minstrel played, and the hand of the Lord came upon His prophet.

Get much alone; but still recollect there is no hope for you if you trust in being alone, or trust in reading the Scriptures, or trust in hearing, or trust in anything but Christ. What you want is the hand of Jesus laid upon you: one touch from Him, and you will be made whole. If you can but touch the hem of His garment, virtue shall come out of Him to you. I am merely mentioning these things because sometimes they lead up to the one thing, and when a man is in earnest to obtain the one thing needful, he will be willing to attend to anything by which he will be likely to attain it, and to attend to any secondary means which God has blessed in the case of others. He will be willing to be taught by a child, if peradventure God will bless him in that manner. He will say, "Bring me a minstrel"; "Bring me a good book"; "Bring me a godly minister"; "Bring me a Christian man accustomed to speak to troubled hearts"; "Bring me an aged Christian whose testimony shall confirm my spirit, and be the means of working faith in me: for I must get to God; I must get salvation." "Tell me, tell me, where Christ is to be obtained, and I will find Him if I ransack the globe to discover Him." I do not believe any person who has desires to find Christ will seek in vain. I am certain that when people hunger and thirst after Christ they shall be filled, and when they say, "We will do anything by which we may be led to Jesus," they are not far from the kingdom of heaven, and the Holy Spirit is at work in them.

III. Thirdly, WE SHOULD MORE ABUNDANTLY USE HOLY

MINSTRELSY. Saints and sinners, too, would find it greatly to their benefit if they said, "Bring me a minstrel." This is the world's cry whenever it is merry, and filled with wine. The art of music has been prostituted to the service of Satan. Charles Wesley well said,—

> "Listed into the cause of sin,
>   Why should a good be evil?
> Music, alas! too long has been
> Press'd to obey the devil.
> Drunken, or lewd, or light, the lay
>   Flow'd to the soul's undoing;
> Widen'd, and strew'd with flowers the way
>   Down to eternal ruin."

It is for us to use singing in the service of God, and to make a conquest of it for our Redeemer. Worldlings want the minstrel to excite them; we want him to calm our hearts and still our spirits. That is his use to us, and we shall do well to employ the harper to that end.

Let us give instances: I will suppose that this morning you were thinking about coming up to the assembly of God's people, and you felt hardly up to the mark. It would have been wise to do as I did this morning. I read at family prayer the eighty-fourth Psalm, "How amiable are thy tabernacles, O Lord of hosts! My soul longeth, yea, even fainteth for the courts of the Lord: my heart and my flesh crieth out for the living God. Yea, the sparrow hath found an house, and the swallow a nest for herself, where she may lay her young, even thine altars, O Lord of hosts, my King, and my God."

What a sweet piece of Sabbath minstrelsy it is! How often have we been quieted and prepared for sanctuary worship by Psalm cxxii:—

> "How did my heart rejoice to hear
>   My friends devoutly say,
> 'In Zion let us all appear
>   And keep Thy holy day!'"

When the house is full of trouble, and your heart is bowed down, is it not well to say—"Bring me a minstrel, and let him sing to me the twenty-seventh Psalm. 'The Lord is my light and my salvation; whom shall I fear? the Lord is the strength of my life; of whom shall I be afraid? When the wicked, even mine enemies and my foes, came upon me to eat up my flesh, they stumbled and fell. Though an host should encamp against me, my heart shall not fear: though war should rise against me, in this will I be confident.'" You need not confine the harper to that one strain; for David has written many psalms for bur-dened hearts. It is wonderful what provision God has made of

sacred minstrels to play us up out of the depths into the heights
if we will but make a right use of them.

I will suppose you are in a state of alarm; it may be there is
a thunderstorm, or possibly a disease is stalking through the
land. Did you ever sing in such times that forty-sixth Psalm:
"God is our refuge and strength, a very present help in trouble.
Therefore will not we fear, though the earth be removed, and
though the mountains be carried into the midst of the sea;
Though the waters thereof roar and be troubled, though the
mountains shake with the swelling thereof. Selah. There is a
river, the streams whereof shall make glad the city of God,
the holy place of the tabernacles of the Most High. God is
in the midst of her; she shall not be moved: God shall help
her, and that right early." Such music is like the breath of
heaven.

How comforting are the words of the ninety-first Psalm when
diseases are abroad, or when the thunder rolls through the
sky: "He that dwelleth in the secret place of the Most High
shall abide under the shadow of the Almighty. I will say of
the Lord, He is my refuge and my fortress: my God; in him
will I trust." I remember being in a family one night when
I was but a lad, when everybody in the house, strong men
though some of them were, trembled and were afraid. A child
was upstairs and must be brought down; but no one dared to
pass by the window on the staircase. Well do I remember fetch-
ing down the child, awed but not alarmed, and then I sat down
and read aloud the ninety-first Psalm, and saw how it quieted
both men and women. Ah, my brethren, David as a musician
is one of a thousand; we need no other minstrel. The word of
God hushes the tempest of the soul, and refreshes the heart
with a celestial dew. "Bring me a minstrel," but let him sing
us one of the songs of Zion.

Do you ever get depressed in spirit, beloved friends? I fear
you do; and are you ever troubled because you seem to have
more affliction than anybody else? Have you watched the
wicked and seen them prosperously sailing while you have
been tossed to and fro on a raging sea of troubles? Do you
want to get peace to your mind by the power of the Holy Spirit?
Then say, "Bring me a minstrel"; and let him sing that thirty-
seventh Psalm, "Fret not thyself because of evildoers." Or if
you would have a change from the thirty-seventh, turn the
figures round, and let him sing the seventy-third, and the notes
will run thus: "Truly God is good to Israel, even to such as
are of a clean heart. But as for me, my feet were almost gone;
my steps had well nigh slipped." You will not be long before
you will rise to the note—"Whom have I in heaven but thee?

and there is none upon earth that I desire beside thee. My flesh and my heart faileth: but God is the strength of my heart, and my portion for ever."

Happily, you are not always depressed: there are times of great joy with you, and then you long to have communion with God. If you wish to have fellowship with Jesus, you will find it helpful to say, "Bring me a minstrel"; and when he asks, "What shall I sing?" say to him, "Sing the Song of Songs, which is Solomon's." Then shall you find utterance for your heart in such canticles as these: "Tell me, O thou whom my soul lovest, where thou feedest, where thou makest thy flock to rest at noon; for why should I be as one that turneth aside by the flocks of thy companions?" Possibly your tongue will take up notes like these: "As the apple tree among the trees of the wood, so is my beloved among the sons. I sat down under his shadow with great delight, and his fruit was sweet to my taste. He brought me to the banqueting house, and his banner over me was love." "My beloved is mine, and I am his: he feedeth among the lilies. Until the daybreak, and the shadows flee away, turn, my beloved, and be thou like a roe or a young hart upon the mountains of division."

When we come to die we will breathe our last breath to music. Then will we say, "Bring me a harper," and like Jacob and Moses we will sing ere we depart. Our song is ready. It is the twenty-third Psalm: "The Lord is my shepherd; I shall not want. Yea, though I walk through the valley of the shadow of death, I will fear no evil: for thou art with me; thy rod and thy staff they comfort me."

This is the kind of minstrel for me. Say you not so, my brethren? When you are in trouble or distress, will you not remember your songs in the night? If such be the strain, I am of the same mind as Martin Luther, whose words I have copied out to read to you. His language is always strong. Luther speaks thunderbolts. "One of the finest and noblest gifts of God is music. This is very hateful to the devil, and with it we may drive off temptations and evil thoughts. After theology I give the next place and highest honours to music. It has often aroused and moved me so that I have won a desire to preach. We ought not to ordain young men to the office of preacher if they have not trained themselves and practised singing in the schools." That is pretty strong. I fear many would not have been preachers if they must first have been singers. Still, there is a power about song; and to sing the praises of God in psalms such as those I have read to you is most consoling.

Suppose you have done with the minstrelsy which I have

now mentioned, there is next *the music of gospel doctrine.* I confess
to you that, when depressed in spirit, I love a bit of thorough
Calvinistic doctrine. I turn to Coles on Divine Sovereignty, and
relish his plain speaking upon sovereign grace. The doctrine of
election is noble music: predestination is a glorious hallelujah.
Grace abounding, love victorious, truth unchanging, faithfulness
invincible: these are melodies such as my ear delights in. The
truth of God is fit music for angels. The harps of the redeemed
never resound with more noble music than the doctrines of
grace. Every truth has its melody, every doctrine is a psalm
unto God. When my heart is faint, "Bring me a minstrel,"
and let him sing of free grace and dying love.

If these do not charm you, fetch a minstrel from *experience.*
Think how God has dealt with you in times of sorrow and
darkness long gone by, and then you will sing, "His mercy
endureth for ever." That one hundred and third Psalm might
last a man from now till he entered heaven, he need not change
the strain,—"Bless the Lord, O my soul: and all that is within
me, bless his holy name." He may keep on chanting it until
his song melts into the hymn of the angels, and he adds another
voice to the chorus of the redeemed above.

If you want music, there is yet a sweeter store. Go fetch a
minstrel *from Calvary.* Commend me for sweetness to the music
of the cross. At Calvary I hear one piece of music set to the
minor key, which has bred more joy beneath the skies than all
else. Hear it: "My God, my God, why hast thou forsaken
me?" Jesus deserted is the comfort of deserted souls: Jesus
crying, "Why hast thou forsaken me?" is the joy of the spirit
that has lost the light of God's countenance. That grave and
solemn note can lift despair into delight.

But if you want another hymn of the cross to be sung with
the accompaniment of the high-sounding cymbals, or with
trumpet and sound of cornet, let me commend you to this other
song of the cross, "IT IS FINISHED." All music lies there. Con-
densed into those three words you have the harmonies of
eternity, the melodies of the infinite. Angels themselves when
on their loftiest key did never sing a canticle so sweet. "*Con-
summatum est*" is the consummation of song. "It is finished";
sin is blotted out, reconciliation is complete, everlasting righteousness is brought in, and believing souls are saved. Hallelujah!
Hallelujah! Till the day break, and the shadows flee away,
"Bring me a minstrel," and let us sing unto Him that loved
us, and washed us from our sins in His own blood, to Him be
glory, for ever and ever. Amen.

THERE GO THE SHIPS

A Sermon

Text.—"There go the ships."—Psalm civ. 26.

I was walking the other day by the side of the sea, looking out upon the English Channel. It so happened that there was a bad wind for the vessels going down the Channel, and they were lying in great numbers between the shore and the Goodwins. I should think I counted more than a hundred, all waiting for a change of wind. On a sudden the wind shifted to a more favourable quarter, and it was interesting to see with what rapidity all sails were spread, and the vessels began to disappear like birds on the wing. It was a sight such as one might not often see, but worth travelling a hundred miles to gaze upon, to see them all sail like a gallant squadron, and disappear southward on their voyages. "There go the ships," was the exclamation that naturally rose to one's lips. The psalmist thought it worth his while to pen the fact which he too had noticed, though it is very questionable whether David had ever seen anything like the number of vessels which pass our coasts, certainly he had seen none to be compared with them for tonnage.

The first lesson which may be learned from the ships and the sea is this—*every part of the earth is made with some design.* The land, of course, yields "grass for the cattle and herb for the service of man"; but what about the broad acres of the sea? We cannot sow them, nor turn them into pasturage. The reaper fills not his arm from the briny furrows, they give neither seed for the sower nor bread for the eater, neither do herds of cattle cover them as they do the thousand hills of earth. Remorselessly swallowing up all that is cast upon it, the thankless ocean makes no return of fruit or flower. Is not the larger part of the world given up to waste? "No," says David, and so say we—"There go the ships." The sea benefits man by occasioning navigation, and yielding besides an enormous harvest of fishes of many kinds. Besides which, as the blood is needful for the body, so is it necessary for this world that there should be upon its surface a vast mass of water in perpetual motion. That measureless gathering together of the waters is an amazing instance of divine wisdom in its existence, its perpetual ebb and flow, and even in its form and quantity. In the ocean there is not a drop of water too much nor a drop too little. There is not a single mile of sea more than there ought to be, nor less than there should be. An exact balance and proportion is maintained, and we little know how the blooming of the tiny flower or the flourishing of the majestic cedar would be affected were the balance disturbed. Between the tiny drop of dew upon each blade of grass and the boundless main there is a relation and proportion such as only an infinite mind could have arranged.

Remember also that the ocean's freshness tends to promote life and health among the sons of men. It is good that there is sea, or the land might devour its inhabitants by sickness. God has made nothing in vain. Ignorance gazes on the stormy deep and judges it to be a vast disorder, the mother of confusion and the nurse of storms; but better knowledge teaches us, what revelation had before proclaimed, namely, that in wisdom has the Lord made all things.

Our subject, however, shall not be the uses of the sea, but this one simple matter—"There go the ships."

I. And, first, WE SEE THAT THE SHIPS GO. "There go the ships." *The ships are made to go.* The ship is not made to lie for ever upon the stocks, or to be shut up in the docks. It is generally looked upon as an old hulk of little service when it has to lie up in ordinary, and rot in the river. But a ship is made to go, and, as you see that it goes, remember that you also were made to go. Activity in Christian work is the result and design of grace in the soul. How I wish we could launch some of you. You are, we trust, converted, but you as yet serve but slender uses, very quiet, sluggish, and motionless you lie on the stocks by the month together, and we have nearly as much trouble to launch you as Brunel had with the "Great Eastern." I have tried hard to knock away your blocks, and remove your dog-shores, and grease your ways, but you need hydraulic rams to stir you. When will you feel that you must go, and learn to "walk the water as a thing of life"? Oh for a grand launch. Hundreds are lying high and dry, and to them I would give the motto, "Launch out into the deep." The ships go, when will you go too?

The ships in going at last disappear from view. The vessel flies before the wind, and very speedily it is gone: and such is our destiny ere long. Our life is gone as the swift ships. We think ourselves stationary, but we are always moving on. As we sit in the pews so quietly the angel of time is bearing us between his wings at a speed more rapid than we guess. Every single tick of the clock is but a vibration of his mighty wings, and he bears us on, and on, and on, and never stays to rest either by day or night. Swift as the arrow from the bow we are always speeding towards the target. How short time is! How very

short our life is! Let each one say, "How short *my* life is!" No
man knows how near he is to his grave. Perhaps if he could
see it, it is just before him: I almost wish he could see it, for
a yawning grave might make some men start to reason and
to thought. That yawning grave is there, though they perceive
it not.

> "A point of time, a moment's space,
> May land me in yon heavenly place,
> Or shut me up in hell."

"There go the ships," and there go you also; you are never
in one stay. You are always flying, swift as the eagle, or, to
come back to the text, as the swift ship, yet "all men think all
men mortal but themselves." The oldest man here probably
thinks he will outlive some of the younger ones. The man who
is soonest to die may be the very man who has the least thought
of death of us all; and he that is nearest to his departure is,
perhaps, the man who least thinks of it. Just as in the ship
all were awake, and every man praying to his God except Jonah,
for whom the storm was raging, so does it often happen that
in a congregation every man may be aroused and made to
think of his latter end except the one man, the marked man,
who will never see to-morrow's sun. As you see the ships, think
of your mortality!

The ships as they go are going on business. Some few ships go
hither and thither upon pleasure, but for the most part the
ships have something serious to do. They have a charter, and
they are bound for a certain port, and this teaches us how we
should go on the voyage of life with a fixed, earnest, weighty
purpose. May I ask each one of you, Have you something to
do, and is it worth doing? You are sailing, but are you sailing
like a mere pleasure yacht, whose port is everywhere, which
scuds and flies before every fitful wind, and is a mere butterfly
with no serious work before it? You may be as heavily laden
and dingy as a collier, there may be nothing of beauty or swift-
ness about you, but after all, the main thing is the practical
result of your voyage.

Dear friend, what are you doing? What have you been doing?
And what do you contemplate doing? I should like every young
man here just to look at himself. Here you are, young man;
you certainly were not sent into this world merely to wear a
coat, and to stand so many feet in your stockings; you must
have been sent here with some intention. A noble creature
like man—and man is a noble creature as compared with the
animal creation—is surely made for something. What were
you made for? Not merely to enjoy yourself. That cannot be.
You certainly are not "a butterfly born in a bower," neither

were you made to be creation's blot and blank. For God's glory we were made. Nothing short of this is worthy of immortal beings. Have we sought that glory? Are we seeking it now?

If any man is obliged to feel that his purpose is such that he dares not avow it, or that he has only existed to make so much money, or gain a position in life, or to enjoy himself, but he has never purposed to serve his God, I would say to him, Wake up, wake up, I pray you, to a noble purpose, worthy of a man. May God, the ever-blessed Spirit, set this before you in the light of eternity, and in the light of Jesus' dying love, and may you be aroused to solemn, earnest purpose and pursuit. "There go the ships," but not idly: they go upon business.

These ships, however, whatever their errand be, *sail upon a changeful sea*. To-day the sea is smooth, like glass: the ship, however, makes very small headway. To-morrow there is a breeze, which fills out the sail, and the ship goes merrily before it. Perhaps, before night comes on, the breeze increases to a gale, and then rushes from a gale into a hurricane. Let the mariner see to it when the storm-winds are out, for the ship need be staunch to meet the tempest. Mark how in the tempestuous hour the sea mingles with the clouds, and the clouds with the sea. See how the ship mounts up to heaven on the crest of the wave, and then dives into the abyss in the furrow between the enormous billows, until the mariners reel to and fro and stagger like drunken men. Anon they have weathered the storm, and perhaps to-morrow it will be calm again. "There go the ships," on an element which is a proverb for fickleness, for we say, "false as the smooth, deceitful sea." "*They* go," say you, "upon the sea, but I dwell upon the solid earth."

Ah, good sir, there is not much to choose. There is nothing stable beneath yon waxing and waning moon. We say "*terra firma*," but where, where is *terra firma?* What man is he who has found out the rock immovable? Certainly not he who looks to this world for it. He has it not who thinks he has, for many plunge from riches into poverty, from honour to disgrace, from power to servitude. Who says "My mountain standeth firm, I shall never be moved"? He speaks as the foolish speak. It is a voyage, sir, and even with Christ on board it is a voyage in which storms will occur, a voyage in which you may have to say, "Master, carest thou not that we perish?" Expect changes, then. Do not hold anything on earth too firmly. Trust in God and be on the watch, for who knoweth what may be on the morrow? "There go the ships."

II. But now having spoken upon that, our second point is, HOW GO THE SHIPS? What makes them go? For there are lessons here for Christian men. We leave our steam ships out of the

question, as they were not known in David's day, and therefore
not intended. But how go the ships? Well, *they must go according
to the wind.* They cannot make headway without favourable
gales. And if our port be heaven, there is no getting there except
by the blessed Spirit's blowing upon us. He bloweth where He
listeth, and we need that He should breathe upon us. We never
steer out of the port of destruction upon our venturesome voyage
till the heavenly wind drives us out to sea; and when we are
out upon the ocean of spiritual life we make no progress unless
we have His favouring breath. We are dependent upon the
Spirit of God, even more than the mariners upon the breeze.
Let us all know this, and therefore cry,

> "Celestial breeze, no longer stay,
> But fill my sails and speed my way."

It is not possible to insist too much on the humbling truth,
"Without me ye can do nothing": it helps to check self-confidence,
and it exalts the Holy Ghost. Unless we honour Him He will
not honour us, and therefore let us cheerfully acknowledge
our absolute dependence upon Him.

*But still the mariner does not go by the wind without exertion on his
own part,* for the sails must be spread and managed so that the
wind may be utilised. One man will go many knots, while another
with the same breeze goes but few, for there is a good deal of
tacking about wanted sometimes, to use the little wind, or the
cross wind, which may prevail. Sometimes all the sails must
be spread, and at other times only a part. Management is
required. If some were spread they might take the wind out
of others, and so the ship might lose instead of gaining. There
is a deal of work on board a ship. I believe that some people
have a notion that the ship goes of itself, and that the sailors
have nothing to do but sit down, and enjoy themselves; but
if you have ever been to sea as an able-bodied seaman, you
have discovered that for an easy life you must not be one of
a ship's crew. And so, mark you, we are dependent upon the
Spirit of God, but He puts us into motion and action; and
if Christian men sit down and say, "Oh, the Spirit of God will
do the work," you will find the Spirit of God will do nothing
of the sort. The only operation which He will be likely to perform
will be to convince you that you are a sluggard, and that you
will come to poverty. The Spirit of God makes men earnest,
fervent, living, and intense. He "works in us to will and to
do of His own good pleasure." We have sails to manage to
catch the favouring breeze, and we shall want all the strength
we can obtain if we are to make good headway in the voyage
of life.

Do you not remember what God said to David? "When thou hearest the sound of a going in the tops of the mulberry trees then shalt thou bestir thyself." Not "Then shalt thou sit still, and say God will do it." When David heard the angels coming over the tops of the trees to fight the Philistines, and when he heard their soft tread amongst the leaves, like the rustling of the wind, then he was to bestir himself: and so, when God's Spirit comes to work in the church, the Christian must bestir himself and not sit still. "There go the ships." They go with the wind, but they are the scene of great industry, or else the wind would whistle through the yards, and the ship would make no voyages. Thus, brethren, we see dependence and energy united; faith sweetly showing itself in good works.

"There go the ships." How do they go? Well, *they have to be guided and steered by the helm.* The helm is a little thing, but yet it rules the vessel. As the helm is turned so is the vessel guided. Look ye well to it, Christian men, that your motives and purposes are always right. Your love is the helm of the vessel; where your affection is your thoughts and actions tend. If you love the world you will drift with the world, but if the love of the Father be in you, then will your vessel go towards God and towards divine things. Oh, see to it that Christ has His hand on the tiller, and that He guides you towards the haven of perfect peace.

The ship being guided by the helm, *he who manages the helm seeks direction from charts and lights.* "There go the ships," but they do not go of themselves, without management and wisdom. Thought is exercised, and knowledge and experience. There is an eye on deck which at night looks out for yonder revolving light, or the coloured ray of the light ship just ahead there, and the thoughtful brain says, "I must steer south-west of such a light," or "to the north of such a light, or I shall be upon the sands." Besides mere outlooks upon the sea, that anxious eye also busies itself with the chart, scans the stars, and takes observations of the moon. The captain's mind is exercised to learn exactly where the vessel is, and where she is going, lest the good ship unawares should come to mischief. And so, dear brethren, if we are to get to heaven, we must study well the Scriptures, we must look well to every warning and guiding light of the Spirit's kindling, and ask for direction from above; for as the ships go not at haphazard, so neither will any Christian find his way to heaven unless he watch and pray and look up daily saying, "Guide me in a plain path, O God."

Once more, how go the ships? They not only go according to the wind, guided by the helm and the chart, but some ships will go better than others, *according to their build.* With the same amount of wind one vessel makes more way than another. Now it is a blessed thing when the grace of God gives a Christian a good build. There are some church members who are so queerly shaped that somehow they never seem to cut the water, and even the Holy Spirit does not make much of them. They will get into harbour at last, but they will need a world of tugging. The snail did get into the ark: I often wonder how he did it, he must have got up very early that morning. However, the snail got in as well as the greyhound, and so there are many Christian people who will get to heaven, but heaven alone knows how, for they are such a queer sort of people that they seem to make no progress in the divine life. I would sooner live in heaven with them for ever than be fifteen minutes with them here below. God seems to shape some Christian minds in a more perfect model than others, so that, having simplicity of character, warmth of heart, zealous temperaments, and generous spirits, when the wind of the Spirit comes they cut through the foam.

Now, I suspect that some good people have by degrees become like the "Great Eastern" a short time since, namely, foul under water. They cannot go, because they are covered with banacles. A ship is greatly impeded in its voyage if it carries a quantity of barnacles on her bottom. I know lots of Christian people —I could point them out to-night, but I will not—who are covered with barnacles. They cannot go, because of some secret inconsistency, or love of the things of this world rather than the love of God. They want laying up and cleaning a bit, so as to get some of the barnacles off. It is a rough process, but it is one to which some of God's vessels have to be exposed. What headway they would make towards heaven if that which hindereth were removed. Sometimes when a man is on a bed of sickness, he is losing his barnacles; and sometimes, when a man has been rich and wealthy, and he has lost all he had, it takes off the barnacles. When we have lost friends we love, and whom we have made idols of, we have been sorry to lose them, but it has cleaned off our barnacles; and when we have got out to sea there has been an ease about the going, and we have scarcely known how it was, but God knew that He had made us more fit for His service by the trials of life to which He exposed us.

That is how the ships go. There are many mysteries about them, and there are many in us. God makes us go by the gales of His Spirit. Oh, that we may be trim for going, buoyant, and swift to be moved, and so may we make a grand voyage to heaven with Christ Jesus at the helm.

III. Thirdly and briefly. When I saw these ships go I happened to be near a station of Lloyd's, and I noticed that they ran up flags as the vessels went by, to which the vessels replied. I suppose they were *asking questions*—to know their names and what their cargo was, and where they were going, and so on. Now I am going to act as Lloyd's to-night, and put up the flags and ask you something about yourselves. The third point will then be—the ships go, LET US SIGNAL THEM.

And, first, *who is your owner?* "There go the ships," but who is your owner? You do not reply, but I think I can make a guess. There are some hypocrites about, who make fine pretensions, but they are not holy living people, they even dare to come to the Lord's table, and yet they drink of the cup of devils. They will sing pious hymns with us, and then sing lascivious ditties with their familiars. I would say to such a man,—you are a rotten vessel, you do not belong to King Jesus. Every timber is staunch in His vessels. They are not all what we should like them to be, and as I have said already they too often are covered with barnacles, but still they are all sincere. The Lord builds His vessels with sound timber, and unless we are sincere, true, and right, Christ is not our owner, but Satan is. The painted hypocrite is known through the disguise he wears.

There is another vessel over there, a fine vessel too. Look, she is newly painted, and looks spick and span. You can see nothing amiss with her. What white sails, and do you notice the many flags? Take the glass and read the vessel's name, and you will see in bold letters, "Self-righteousness." Ah, I know that the owner is not the Lord Jesus Christ, for all the ships that belong to Him carry the red cross flag, and cannot endure the flaunting rag of self-righteousness. All God's people own that they must be saved by sovereign grace, and anything like righteousness of their own they pump overboard as so much leakage and bilge-water.

I see another vessel over yonder, with her sails all spread, and every bit of her colours flying. There, there, what a blaze she makes! How proud she seems as she scuds over the water. That vessel is "The Pride," from the port of Self-Conceit, Captain Ignorance. I do not know where she is oftenest to be seen, but sometimes she crosses this bit of water. I should not wonder if she is in sight here now, and you may be sure she does not belong to our Lord Jesus. Whether it is pride of money, or person, or rank, or talent, it cometh of evil, and Jesus Christ does not own it. You must get rid of all pride if you belong to Him. God grant us to be humble in heart.

I could mention some more vessels that I see here to-night, but I will not. I will rather beg each man to ask himself, "Can

I put my hand on my heart and say, 'I am not my own, I am bought with a price?' Did Jesus buy me with His precious blood, and do I own that there is not a timber, spar, rope, or bolt in me but what belongs to Him?" Blessed be His name, some of us can say there is not a hair of our head or a drop of our blood but what belongs to Him. Thine are we, Thou Son of David, and all that we have.

I hope there are vessels here which are owned by the Lord Jesus Christ. Let them never be ashamed to confess their Owner. A vessel on proper business is never ashamed to answer signals. If there should be a smuggler or pirate in the offing the crews would not be likely to answer signals, but those who are on honest business are ready to reply. And so, brethren, be ye ready to give a reason for the hope that is in you with meekness and fear; never show in your actions that you are ashamed of Jesus, but ever let the broad flag be flying in whatever waters you are—"Christ is mine, and I am His. For Him I live, His reproach would I bear, and His honour would I maintain."

Our next inquiry is, *what is your cargo?* "There go the ships," but what do they carry? You cannot tell from looking at them far out at sea, except that you can be pretty sure that some of them do not carry much. Look at that showy brig! You can tell by the look of her that she has not much on board; from the fact of her floating so high it is clear that her cargo is light. Big men, very important individuals, very high-floating people are common, but there is nothing in them. If they had more on board they would sink deeper in the water. The more grace a man has the lower he lies before God. Well, brethren, what cargo have you got? I am afraid some of you who lie down in the water are not kept down by any very precious cargo, but I fear you are in ballast. I have gone aboard some Christians; I thought there was a good deal in them, but I have not been able to find it. They have a deal of trouble, and they always tell you about it. There is a good old soul I call in to see sometimes: I begin to converse with her, and her conversation is always about rheumatism: nothing else: you cannot get beyond rheumatism: that good sister is in ballast. There is another friend of mine, a farmer, if you talk with him, it is always about the badness of the times: that brother is in ballast too. There are many tradesmen who, though they are Christians, cannot be made to talk of anything but the present dulness of business. I wish they could get that ballast out, and fill up with something better; for it is not worth carrying. You must have it sometimes, I suppose; but it is infinitely better to carry a load of praises, prayers, good wishes, holy doctrines, charitable actions, and generous encouragements.

Some ships, I think, carry a cargo of *powder*. You cannot go very near them without feeling you are in danger, they are so very apt to misjudge and take offence. I wish that such persons were made to carry a red flag, that we might give them a wide berth.

It is well to be loaded with good things. Young people, study the word of God, ask to be taught by experience, and, wherever you go, seek to carry the precious commodities which God has made dear to your own soul, that others may be enriched thereby. It is an interesting sight to see those immense ships loaded with passengers for the colonies. Thank God, I have sometimes had my decks crowded with passengers who have from my ministry received the gospel. The Lord has brought them on board, and oh, I trust before I die He will give me thousands more who will have to thank God that they heard the gospel from these lips. May we be emigrant vessels bearing souls away into the glory-land where the days of their mourning shall be ended. Of course we can only be humble instruments, but still, what honour God puts upon His instruments when He makes use of them for this object. "There go the ships." Not ships of war are we, with guns to carry death, but missionary vessels carrying tidings of peace and glad news to the utmost ends of the earth.

Our last signal asks the question—*where go the ships?* Where go the ships? Oh, yes, they went merrily down the Channel the other day, but where are they now? In a year's time who will report all the good vessels which just now passed by our coast? I am looking out upon all of you, anxious to know what port you are making for. Some of you are bound for the port of peace. Swiftly may the winds convey you over the waters, and safely may you voyage under the convoy of the Lord Jesus. I will try and keep pace with you. I hope that you will sail in company with others of my Master's vessels, but if you have to sail alone over a sea in which you cannot see another sail, may God, the blessed One, protect and guard you. Bound for the port of peace, with Christ on board, insured for glory, bound for life eternal, let us bless the name of the Lord.

But alas, alas, many ships which bid fair for the desired haven are lost on the rocks. Some soul-destroying sin causes their swift destruction. Others equally fair to look upon are lost on the sands. They seemed bound for heaven, but they were not the Lord's. The sands are very dangerous, but they are only a mass of little atoms, soft and yielding, yet as many ships are lost on the sands as on the rocks. Even so there are ways and habits of evil which are deceptive—there is nothing very bad about them apparently; nothing heart-breaking, like rocks, but oh, the multitudes of souls that have been sucked in by sandy temptations. Dear brother, I hope you are not going that way. God grant you grace to avoid little sins, and I am sure you will keep off the rocks of great sin. In any case may we turn out to be the Lord's own, and so be kept to the end. Woe unto us if we should prove to be mere adventurers, and perish in our presumption.

Among the ships that go to sea there are some that *founder*. One does not know how, but they are never heard of more. They were sighted on such a day, but never more shall we hear any tidings of them. How is that? I have known some of the members of this church go down in mid-ocean. I never thought it could have happened, but they have gone. I can only imagine how it was. They seemed seaworthy vessels, but they were doubtless rotten through and through. Oh, brethren, may God keep you from foundering, as some do by some mysterious sin, which seems as if it clasped the soul and dragged it down to the deeps of hell.

Some vessels have I known, too, that have become *derelict*— waifs and strays upon the sea—men that were the hope of churches, but who have abandoned themselves to reckless living. They used to worship with the people of God, and seemed to be very earnest and zealous; and now, perhaps, at this very moment they are passing through the gin palace door, or spending this evening in vices which we dare not mention. Oh, it is dreadful. Many start on their voyage, and look as if they were Christ's own vessels, and yet for some strange, unreasonable reason they give it all up, and they will be met with, in years to come, drifting about, rudderless, captainless, crewless, dangerous to others, and miserable to themselves. God save you from this, young man!

Where will some of the vessels I see before me go? It is a fine fleet I am looking upon. Brothers and sisters, I hope all of us will be found in that great harbour in heaven which can accommodate all His Majesty's fleet. Oh, it will be a great day when we all arrive. Will you give me a hail when you get into port? Will you know me? I shall look out for some of you. I cannot help believing that we shall know each other. How we will glorify Him Who gets us there, even Jesus, the Lord High Admiral of the seas. Christ shall never hear the last of it if I get to heaven. *I will* sing, yea, I will sing praises unto His name. I remember preaching once, when half of my congregation quarrelled with me when I had done preaching, for I had said—

> "Then loudest of the crowd I'll sing
> While heaven's resounding mansions ring
> With shouts of sovereign grace."

As I came downstairs I met one who said, "You will not sing loudest, for I owe more to grace than you do"; and I found that all the Lord's people said the same. Well, we will have it out when we get to heaven: we will try this contention among the birds of Paradise, and see which of us can sing the most loudly to the praise of redeeming grace. Till then let us trust the Lord Jesus and obey His orders, for He is our Captain, and it is our duty to do His bidding.

But it would be a dreadful supposition—and yet, mayhap, it may be worse than a supposition—that some of you will have to cast anchor for ever in the Dead Sea, whose waves are fire, where every vessel is a prison, where every passenger feels a hell. What must it be to be in hell an hour! I wish some of you could think it over. What must it be to be shut up in despair for one single day! If you have the toothache a few minutes how wretched you are, and how anxious to get rid of it; but what must it be to be in hell even if it were for a time,—even it were *but* for a time.

Oh, if it came to an end, still would I say, by all the humanities that are in my soul, I charge you, brother, do not risk the wrath of God; go not down to the pit. Pull down that black flag, man: pull it down and cast off your old owner. Ask Christ to be your owner. Run up the red flag of the cross and give yourself to Jesus, for if you do not your voyage must lead to the gulf of black despair, where you will suffer for ever the result of your sin. God have mercy upon us, and may we never have to pass through the straits of judgment into the gulf of damnation. May it never be said, "There goes one of the ships that the Tabernacle pilot signalled; it is gone to destruction." May it rather be said, of all of us, all in full sail together, as we go towards heaven, "There go the ships": not one of them is drifting to the gulf of destruction. Believe in the Lord Jesus Christ, and all is well with you. Reject Him, and all is ill with you. May He by His word enable you to make a right choice to-night, for His love's sake. Amen.

JESUS KNEW WHAT HE WOULD DO

A Sermon

Text.—"This he said to prove him: for he himself knew what he would do."—John vi. 6.

Observe, dear friends, how careful the Holy Spirit is that we should not make a mistake about our Lord Jesus Christ. He knew that men are liable to think too little of the ever blessed Son of God, and that some, who call themselves Christians, nevertheless deny Christ's divinity, and are ever ready to forge an argument against the true and real deity of the Saviour out of anything which appears to limit His power or knowledge. Here is an instance of the care of the Spirit to prevent our falling into an erroneous conclusion. Our Lord consults with Philip, asking this poor disciple, "Whence shall we buy bread, that these may eat?" Some might therefore have inferred that Jesus did not know what to do, but felt embarrassed. From this they would argue that Jesus cannot be Almighty God, for surely embarrassment is inconsistent with Omnipotence. Why should Jesus consult with Philip if He knows all things?

Now, the Holy Spirit would have us beware of falling into low thoughts of our great Redeemer and Lord, and especially of ever being so mistaken as to think that He is not God; therefore He plainly tells us, "this he said to prove Philip, for he himself knew what he would do." Jesus was not asking information or taking counsel with Philip because He felt any doubt about His line of procedure, or needed help from His disciple. He did not want Philip to multiply bread, but He desired to multiply Philip's faith. Take heed, therefore, dear friends, that you never think little of the Saviour, or impute any of His acts to motives that would lessen His glory.

Learn here, too, that we, being very apt to make mistakes concerning Christ, need daily that the Spirit of God should interpret Christ to us. Jesus simply asks the question of Philip "Whence shall we buy bread?" and we are at once in danger of drawing a wrong inference, and therefore the Holy Spirit tells us more about Christ that we may escape from that danger. By giving us more insight into our Lord's motives, He prevents our misjudging His actions. We must have the Spirit of God with us, or we shall not know Christ Himself. The only way to see the sun is by its own light; and the only way to see Jesus

31

is by His own Spirit. Did He not Himself say, "He shall receive of mine, and shall shew it unto you"? No man can call Jesus "Lord" but by the Holy Ghost. The Spirit must come to each man personally, and reveal the Son of God to him, and in him. Therefore, do not let us take up the Bible and imagine that we shall at once understand it as we do another book, but let us breathe the prayer that the Great Author of its letter would Himself give us grace to enter into its spirit, so as to know its meaning and feel its power.

Even with the infallible word before you, you will miss your way, and fall into grievous error unless you are taught of God. The mercy is that it is written, "All thy children shall be taught of the Lord"; and again, "We have an unction from the Holy One, and know all things." There is no knowing anything except by that unction, and by that divine teaching. What dependent creatures we are, since we make mistakes even about Jesus Christ Himself unless the Spirit of God is pleased to instruct us concerning Him! Lead us ever, O light of God!

Another thing we learn from the text before we plunge into it is, that our divine Lord always has a reason for everything that He does. Even the reason of His asking a question may be found out; or, if we cannot discover it, we may still be quite sure that there is a worthy reason. That reason in Philip's case certainly was not because of any want of wisdom in Himself, but there was a reason,—"This he said to prove him." Now, if there is a reason for all that Jesus asks, much more is there a reason for all that He does. In the matter of your present trial and trouble, dear friend you have been trying to spell out the design of the Almighty, but without success. Know you not that His ways are past finding out? In all probability this side of eternity you may never discover God's purpose in your present trial, but that He has a purpose is certain, and that purpose is a wise and kind one. It is such as you yourself would delight in if you were capable of understanding it.

If you could have a mind like that of God, you would act as God does even in this matter which troubles you: at present your thoughts are far below those of God, and therefore you err when you try to measure His ways. Do believe in your Lord, and be quieted: Jesus knows what He is doing, and why He is doing it. For the loss of your health there is a reason. For those pains of body, for that depression of spirit, for that want of success in business, even for the permission of the cruel tongue of slander to inflict its wounds upon you, there is a reason; and possibly that reason may lie in the words of our text, "This he did to prove him." You must be tested. God does not give faith, or love, or hope, or any grace without meaning to prove it.

Let us at once come to the text, which seems to me to have much comfort in it. May the Holy Spirit lead us into it.

First, here is *a question for Philip*—"Whence shall we buy bread, that these may eat?"—a question with a purpose. But, secondly, there is *no question with the Master*, for He Himself knew what He would do. And, thirdly, if we enter into the spirit of the Master there will be *an end of questions with us*, for we shall be perfectly satisfied that He knows what He is going to do.

I. First, then, HERE IS A QUESTION FOR PHILIP, as there have been many questions for us. Jesus put this question to Philip *with the motive of proving him* in several points. He would thus try his *faith*. As one has well said, "He wanted not food of Philip, but faith." The Master enquires, "Whence shall we buy bread, that these may eat?" What will Philip say? If Philip has strong faith he will answer, "Great Master, there is no need to buy bread; Thou art greater than Moses, and under Moses the people were fed with manna in the wilderness; Thou hast but to speak the word, and bread shall be rained around the host, and they shall be filled." If Philip had possessed great faith he might have replied, "Thou art greater than Elisha, and Elisha took a few loaves and ears of corn and fed therewith the sons of the prophets. O wonder-working Lord, Thou canst do the same."

If Philip had displayed greater faith still, he might have said, "Lord, I do not know where bread is to be bought, but it is written, 'Man shall not live by bread alone.' Thou canst refresh these people without visible bread. Thou canst satisfy their hunger and fill them to the full, and yet they need not eat a single mouthful; for it is written, 'By every word that proceedeth out of the mouth of God shall man live.' Speak Thou the word, and they will be at once refreshed." This question, therefore, was put to prove Philip's faith. It did prove it, and proved it to be very little, for he began calculating his pennyworths—"One, two, three, four." No; I will not count two hundred; but that is what Philip did. He began counting pennies, instead of reckoning on Omnipotence. Did you ever do the same, dear friend, when you have been tried? Did you get reckoning up and counting coppers, instead of looking to the eternal God and trusting in Him? I fear that few of us can plead exemption from this failure.

The question was meant, no doubt, to prove Philip's *love*, and he could endure that test better than he could stand the other; for he loved Jesus even though he was slow of heart to believe. In many true hearts there is more quiet love than active faith. I am sorry that there should be little faith, but thankful that there should be more love. The Saviour seemed to say, "Philip, I want these people fed. Will you come to My help in it? Whence shall *we* buy bread? I am going to associate you with Me, Philip. Come, now, how shall *we* do the work?" Philip loves his Master, and therefore he is quite ready to consider the matter, and to give at least the benefit of his arithmetic. He says, "Lord, two hundred pennyworth is not sufficient." His Master did not ask him what would *not* be sufficient, but what would be; but Philip begins calculating the negative question—which question I also am afraid that you and I have often calculated.

Even to give each one in the crowd a little could not be done under two hundred pence; is it not clear that our resources are inadequate? That is always a depressing and unpractical question to go into. Poor Philip counts up what would *not* be sufficient for all, and leaves the Lord all-sufficient out of the reckoning. Still, even in that calculation he showed his love for his Master. It will be well for us to love our Lord so much that we never speak of His gracious plans as being visionary, nor judge them to be impossible. Jesus never proposes Quixotic schemes, and we must never allow the idea to cross our minds: even the conquest of the world to truth and righteousness is not to be looked upon as a dream, but to be practically considered.

The question also tried Philip's *sympathy*. Jesus by this query moved Philip's heart to care about the people. The other disciples said, "Send the multitude away, that they may go into the villages and buy themselves victuals." Jesus, perhaps, noticing a little more tenderness in Philip than in the others, said to Philip, "Whence shall we buy bread?" It was putting great honour upon Philip to associate him with Himself; but perhaps He saw in him a sympathetic soul, and Christ loves to work with sympathetic agents. One thing I notice—that God seldom uses greatly a man who has a hard heart, or a cold heart. Warmth within ourselves can alone create warmth in others. A man must love people or he cannot save them. A minister must have an intense desire that his congregation should be saved, and must get into sympathy with Jesus upon that subject, or else Jesus will not make use of him.

But why was that question put *to Philip*? Why is a special question put to some one of you, or a peculiar trial sent to one of you? It was sent to prove him it is said; but why to prove *Philip*?

Well, I think the Saviour spoke to Philip because Philip was of Bethsaida. They were near Bethsaida, and so Jesus said to Philip, "Whence shall we buy bread?" Every man should think most of the place where he lives. I want Jesus to say to some of you, "What shall we do for London?"—because many of you are Londoners—possibly born within the sound of Bow bells, or within the postal district. If the Lord does lay London on anybody's hearts, He would naturally lay it upon the hearts of those who live in it; just as He said to Philip, "Whence shall we buy bread?" If He associates anybody with Himself in the evangelization of a village or town, it will naturally be a person either born there, or living there. I know that the old proverb declares that the cobbler's wife goes barefoot, and sometimes a man will care for people thousands of miles away, and not look to his own house, or to his own neighbourhood, but it should not be so, for it is to Philip, the Bethsaida man, that the message comes about the people when they are near Bethsaida— "Whence shall we buy bread?" It is said to prove him and to you, brother Londoner, questions about this great city are sent to prove you.

And perhaps it came to Philip because he was not quite so forward in the school of grace as some were. Philip did not make a very wise remark when he said, "Show us the Father, and it sufficeth us," for our Lord answered, "Have I been so long time with you, and yet hast thou not known me, Philip?" He was evidently slow in learning. I do not think that Philip was the most stupid of the twelve, but I am sure that he was not the most intelligent. James and John and Peter were the first three: Andrew and Thomas followed close behind, and probably Philip was close after them. Perhaps Philip was number six; I do not know; but certainly the Saviour selected him as not the lowest in the class, yet not the highest, and He said to him, "Whence shall we buy bread?"

These people in the middle position very much want proving for their own satisfaction. The lowest kind of Christians are so feeble that they can hardly bear proving. Poor souls, they need encouraging rather than testing, and therefore the greatest problems are not often pressed upon them. On the other hand, the highest kind of Christians do not so much require testing, for they make their calling and election sure. The middle sort most need proving, and they make up, I am afraid, the great bulk of the rank and file of the army of God. How many there are who may be described as half instructed, half enlightened, and to these the Lord puts the question, "Whence shall we buy bread?" This He says that He may prove them.

Note well that *the question which the Saviour put to Philip to prove him answered its purpose*. It did prove him. How it proved him

I have shown you already. It answered its purpose because it revealed his inability. "Whence shall we buy bread?" Philip gives it up. He has made a calculation of what would *not* suffice even to give every man a little refreshment, and that is all his contribution to the work: he has not even a loaf or a fish which he can produce to make a start with. Philip is beaten. What is more, his faith, being proved, is beaten too. "Oh, good Master," he seems to say, "the people cannot be fed by us. *We* cannot buy bread—we—not even you and I. Thou art the Lord, and Thou canst do great things; yet my faith is not strong enough to believe that *we* could buy bread enough for all these thousands of people." So the question answered its purpose. It tested Philip's faith, and his faith was proved to be very weak, very wavering, very short-handed. Is it a good thing to find that out? Yes, brethren, it is good to know our spiritual poverty. Many of us have a heap of faith, as we think, but if the Lord were to prove it, He would not need to put it *in* the fire to melt it; He has only to put it *on* the fire, and the most of it would evaporate. Under ordinary trial much faith disappears like morning dew when the sun looks upon it.

What a deal of faith a man has when he is healthy! Just turn on the screw and let him suffer. See how much of that faith will vanish. How many men have faith if they have an excellent income regularly paid; but when they have to ask, "Where will the next meal come from?" have they faith? Alas, they grow anxious and cumbered. It is a wholesome thing to be made to see what weaklings we are, for when we find much of our faith to be unreal, it drives us to seek for more true faith, and we cry, "Lord, increase our faith." Philip was drawn into his Master; and it is a grand thing to be driven right out of ourselves to our Lord so as to feel, "Lord, I cannot do it; but I long to see how Thou wilt perform Thy purpose. I cannot even believe in Thee as I ought to believe, unless Thou givest me faith, so that even for more faith I must come to Thee. Quite empty handed I must come and borrow everything." Then it is that we become full and strong. You will see Philip breaking the bread directly, and feeding the multitude just because Christ has emptied Philip's hands. Until He has emptied our hands He cannot fill them, lest it should be supposed that we shared in the supplying. "This he said to prove him," to make him see his own weakness, for then he should be filled with the Master's strength.

This question did good, for *it was meant not only to prove Philip but to prove the other disciples*, and so they came together, and they had a little talk upon the subject. At any rate, here is a committee of two—Philip and Andrew. Philip says, "Two hundred pennyworth is not sufficient," and Andrew says, "Well no, it is not; but there is a lad here with five barley loaves, and two small fishes." I like this brotherly consultation of willing minds, and to see how they differ in their ideas. Philip is willing to begin if he has a grand start; he must see at least two hundred pennyworth of bread in hand, and then he is ready to entertain the idea. Andrew, on the other hand, is willing to commence with a small capital; a few loaves and fishes will enable him to start, but he remarks, "What are they among so many?"

When saints converse together they help each other, and perhaps what one does not discover another may. Philip was counting the impossible pence, and could not see the possible loaves: but Andrew could see what Philip overlooked. He spied out the lad with that basket packed full of loaves and fishes. It was not much: Andrew had not faith enough to see food for the thousands in that little basket; but still he saw what he did see, and he told the Master of it. Thus they made a commencement by mutual consultation; perhaps if we were to consult we might make a start too. When a question eats into men's hearts like this—"What shall we do for London?" when it leads Christian people to come together and talk about it, and when one sighs out, "Why, it will take many thousands to build chapels, and find ministers, and maintain missionaries," there is something hopeful in the calculation. All right, Philip, I am glad you have had your say, and shown the difficulty of the task. And then I like Andrew to get up and say, "It is a very difficult task, but still we must do what we can do, and as we have these five loaves and two small fishes we must at least put these before the Lord, and leave it with Him as to what is to be done." All this is better than shirking the question altogether, and leaving the crowd to starve.

Philip had his faculties exercised. Christ tried his arithmetic; He tried his eyesight; He tried his mind and spirit; and this prepared him to go and serve at the monster banquet which followed. A man never does a thing well till he has thought about it; and if Philip had not thought about how to feed the multitudes he would not have been a fit man to be employed in it. It prepared him also to adore his Master after the feast, for Philip would say when the meal was over, "The Master asked me how it was to be done, but I could not tell Him, and now, though I have had a share in doing it, He must and shall have all the glory. He multiplied the fishes, and increased the loaves. My poor faith can take no glory to itself. He did it. He did it all." Perhaps some question comes to you, my brother, about the Lord's work—"How can it be done? How can England be evangelized? How can the masses be reached?

How can the world be made to hear the gospel?" Whatever the question is which is put to you, it is a question sent on purpose to do you good, and benefit your soul, and to lead you to magnify the Lord all the more when the miracle of grace is done.

II. Now I come to the second part of the subject, and that is, that THERE WAS NO QUESTION WITH JESUS. The question was with Philip, but Christ had no question: "This he said to prove him: for he himself knew what he would do."

Let us take these words and pull them to pieces a minute. "*He knew.*" He always does know. "Ah," says one, "I am sure I do not know what I shall do." No, dear friend, and yet you have been taking advice, have you not? That is a splendid way of confusing yourself. I hear you cry in bewilderment, "I do not know. I have been to everybody, and I do not know what I shall do." That is a chronic state with us when we puzzle our own poor brains; but Jesus knew what He would do. This is sweet comfort; Jesus knows. He always knows all about it. He knew how many people there were. He knew how much bread it would take: he knew how many fish He would want, and how He meant to feed the crowd, and send them all away refreshed. He knew all before it happened.

Tried brother, Jesus knows all about *your* case and how He is going to bring *you* through. Do not think that you can inform Him as to anything. "Your heavenly Father knoweth what ye have need of before ye ask him." Prayer is not meant for the Lord's information. The question is not put to you that you may instruct Him, but that He may instruct you. He made the heavens and the earth without you. With whom took He counsel? Who instructed Him? And He will bring you through this present trial of yours without needing to add your poor wisdom to His infinite knowledge. He knows.

Jesus *knew what He would do.* He meant to do something; He was quite ready to do it; and He knew what He was going to do. We embarrass ourselves by saying, "Something must be done, but I do not know who is to do it." The Saviour knew that something must be done, and He knew that He was going to do it Himself. He was not in a hurry, He never is: "He never is before His time, He never is too late." Our blessed Master has glorious leisure, because He is always punctual. Late people are in a hurry; but He, being never late, never hurries. He does everything calmly and serenely, because He foresees what He will do. Jesus knows, dear friend, concerning you, not only what you will do, but what He will do. That is the point, and He means to do some great thing for you and to help you. He means also to bring this city and this nation

to His feet. He means that every knee shall bow to Him, and
that the whole earth shall be filled with His glory. He knows
what He means to do.

He knew, moreover, *how He meant to do it*. He knew precisely
the way and method which He intended to use. He perceived
long before Andrew told Him that there was a lad somewhere
in the crowd with five barley cakes. When the lad set out that
morning, I cannot make out what made him bring five barley
loaves and fishes into that crowd; except the Master had whis-
pered in his heart, "Young lad, take with you a good lunch.
Put those barley cakes into the basket, and do not forget the
fishes. You do not know how long you may be from home."
Nature bade him provide for contingencies, but then nature is
God's voice when He chooses to make it so. He was a hungry,
growing lad with a fine appetite, and he meant to be well provided for; but had he ever thought in his mind that these strangely
providential cakes would multiply so as to feed that mass of
people? Where is the man that is to be the universal provider?
Where is the chief of the commissariat? It is that youth, and
that is the whole of his storehouse. He is carrying a magazine
of victuals on his back—in that basket. The Saviour knew that.
And He knows exactly, dear friend, where your help is to come
from in your hour of trouble. You do now know, but He
does.

Once more, *He did it as one who knew what He was going to do.*
How does a man act when he knows what he is going to do?
Well, he generally proceeds in the most *natural* way. He knows
that he is going to do it; so he just goes and does it. Can you
conceive that a miracle was ever performed in a more natural
style? If this had been a Roman Catholic miracle, they would
have thrown the loaves up in the air, and they would have
come down mysteriously transformed and multiplied a million
times; all popish miracles, if you observe, have a great deal of
the theatrical and showy about them. They are totally distinct
from the miracles of Christ. He does this miracle in the most
natural way in the world, because it is virtually the same miracle
which Christ works every year. We take a certain quantity of
wheat, and put it into the ground, and, in the long run, the
end of it is that it is multiplied into loaves of bread. Certain
fishes are in the sea, and they increase into great shoals. The
sown wheat passes through the same operation in the ground
in the same hands—in God's hands, but it comes out loaves of
bread; and that is precisely what came of our Lord's action.
He took a little into His own blessed hands, and brake it, and
it kept on multiplying in His hands, and in the hands of His
disciples, till they were all filled.

He knew what He was going to do, and so He did it naturally and did it *orderly*. It is not so when a man does not know what he is to provide for. We have a large meeting, and there is provision made for tea, and three times as many come as you have provided for. What a hurry! What a scurry! What a running to and fro! Jesus never conducts His matters in that way. He knew what He was going to do, and, therefore, He bade the men sit down on the grass; and they sat down like so many children. Mark tells us that they sat down in rows by fifties and by hundreds; they were arranged as if each one had been specially set to his plate, and found his name laid upon it. Moreover, there was much grass in the place, so that the hall was carpeted in a way that no firm in London could have done it. The feast was conducted as orderly as if there had been notice given seven days beforehand, and a contractor had supplied the provisions. Nothing could have been done in a better way, and all because Jesus knew what He would do.

Moreover, He did it very *joyfully*. He took bread and blessed it. He went about it with great pleasure. I should have liked to have seen His face as He looked on these poor famishing people being fed. Like a good host, He cheered them with His smile, while He blessed them with the food.

And then He did it so *plentifully*, for He knew what He would do; so He did not come half provided, or stint them so that every man should have "a little." No; He knew what He would do, and He measured their appetites exactly, a difficult thing when you have a number of hungry people to feed. He provided all that they wanted, and afterwards there was provision left for the head waiters, so that each one should have a basketful for himself; for they took up of the fragments twelve basketfuls— one for each of the head waiters.

Our Lord Jesus Christ, in the matter of bringing in His own elect, is going about it, I am quite certain, knowing what He is going to do; and when you and I see the end of the great festival of mercy we shall say, "Blessed be the Lord! We were in a great worry; we were in sore trouble; but our Lord has done it easily, and thoroughly. There has been no muddle, no crowding, no passing over of anybody. Blessed be His name! He has not done it by chance or through fortunate circumstances; but He knew what He would do, and He has planned it all through from the beginning to the end in such a way that principalities and powers in heaven shall sing for ever of the grace and love and wisdom and power and prudence wherein He has abounded towards His people." Oh, but if we could see the end as well as the beginning we should begin even now to exalt the name of Jesus our Saviour, who foreknows all His work, and never deviates from His plan.

III. I conclude by saying that because there is no question with Christ, though He puts questions to us, THERE OUGHT TO BE NO QUESTION OF A DOUBTFUL CHARACTER ANY LONGER TO US. Let me mention three questions and I have done.

The first question that troubles a great many people is, "*How shall I bear my present burden?* How shall I endure this suffering? How shall I get a living?" That question is sent to you to prove you; but do remember that there is no question with Christ as to how you will get through, for "as thy day so shall thy strength be," and He will keep His saints, even to the end. Therefore let there be no question with you, for Jesus Himself knows what He will do. You came here to-night very distressed, and you said, "I wish I might get a word to tell me what I should do." You will not get half a word as to what *you* shall do, but you shall hear a word of a different sort. Jesus knows what HE will do; and what He will do is infinitely better than anything you can do. Your strength, my friend, is to sit still. Roll your burden upon the Lord. Do the little you can do, and leave the rest with your heavenly Father. This is the answer from the Urim and the Thummim for you,—Jesus knows what He will do.

There is that other question, which I have already mooted: *What is to be done with this great city?* I had the great privilege of being able to preach yesterday afternoon in one of our eastern suburbs, and setting out from my own house early in the morning, I went on riding, riding, upon one railway and another till I think I must have been journeying for fully two hours and a half before I had passed from one end of London to another. What a city of magnificent distances! And, then, as you go along with a Christian friend, he says, "There is a chapel wanted here." Or "There is a little chapel here, but not one person in fifty goes to a place of worship." Then you arrive at another suburban place, and your guide will say, "Here are people anxious for the gospel, but there is nobody to take it to them." I went along yesterday sorely burdened, and questioning in my heart, "What shall we do?" O that we had men and money to send out ministers and to build places for them to preach in. Surely many of you must have been burdened with the hugeness of this city. But, dear, dear, this is like one drop of rain in a great shower compared with the whole world that lieth in the wicked one. How is this world to be enlightened? It is no question with Jesus, and, therefore, it should never be an unbelieving question with us. "Can these dry bones live?" Let us answer "Lord, Thou knowest." There will we leave it. He is able to do exceeding abundantly above what we ask, or even think, and we may depend upon it that if He has sworn by Himself that every knee shall bow, and every tongue confess to Him, it shall be so, and He shall have the glory.

One other question should be mentioned. It is this. Has the Lord put into the heart of any unconverted person the question, —" *What must I do to be saved?* " And is that question perplexing any of you? I am glad it is so, but I hope you will turn to the right place for an answer. I hope you are enquiring,—Lord, what wouldst Thou have *me* to do? Do you know why that question is put to you? It is to prove you, and to humble you. It is meant to make you feel the impossibility of salvation by your own works, that you may submit yourself to the righteousness of God, and be saved by faith in Christ Jesus. Remember that there is no question with Christ about how you are to be saved. In fact, that question was settled—when shall I say? Settled when He died? No, settled long before that: it was decided in the everlasting covenant before the day-star knew its place, or planets ran their round. God had then regarded His Son as the Lamb of God, slain before the foundation of the world, and to this day the word still stands—"Behold the Lamb of God, which taketh away the sin of the world." Look unto Him and be saved.

There is no question about the possibility of your salvation, or about Christ's ability to save you. The question in your heart, "What must I do to be saved?" is put there to prove you; but Jesus Himself knows what He will do. What a blessed word is that! He knows how He will pardon, comfort, regenerate, instruct, and lead you. He knows how He will keep you to the end by His unchanging grace. He knows how He will preserve you, and sanctify you, and use you, and glorify His own name by you, and take you up to heaven, and set you upon His throne, and make all the angels wonder and adore, as they see what He will do. God bless you for Jesu's sake. Amen.

AMONG LIONS

A Sermon

Text.—"My soul is among lions."—Psalm lvii. 4.

SOME of you cannot say this, and you ought to be very thankful that you are not obliged to do so. Happy are you young people who have godly parents, and who dwell in Christian families. You ought to grow like the flowers in a conservatory, where killing frosts and biting blasts are unknown. You live under very favourable circumstances. Your soul, I might almost say, is among angels; for you dwell where God is worshipped, where family prayer is not forgotten, where you can have a kindly guidance in the hour of difficulty and comfort in the time of trial. You dwell where angels come and go, and God Himself deigns to dwell. Happy young people to be thus circumstanced! How grateful and how holy you ought to be! I want all who dwell where everything helps them to recollect the many gracious ones who dwell where everything hinders them. You who live near the Beautiful Gate of the temple must not forget the many who are sighing in the tents of Kedar. If your soul is not among lions, praise God for it; and then let your sympathies go out towards those who mournfully complain—

> "My soul with him that hateth peace
> Hath long a dweller been;
> I am for peace; but when I speak,
> For battle they are keen."

It is a Christian duty to "remember them that are in bonds as bound with them"; and whenever our own favoured circumstances lead us to forget those who are persecuted and tried, our very mercies are working mischief to us. "We are all members one of another." If one member suffers, all the rest should suffer with him; and therefore, we will turn our thoughts towards our persecuted brethren to-night, that our united supplications may sustain them under their difficulties, and, if the Lord be so pleased, may even deliver them.

When may a Christian man truly say, "My soul is among lions"? Such is the case when, either from our being members of ungodly families, or from having to gain our livelihood amongst unconverted and graceless people, we are subjected to reproach and rebuke, and to jest and jeer for Jesus Christ's sake. Then we can say, "My soul is among lions." Many in this congregation known to me are the only ones in their family whom God has called. I bless His name that He is often taking one of a household, and a lone one of a family, and bringing such to Jesus. Some quite un-Christian person who thinks not of God drops in here out of curiosity, and God meets with him and he becomes the first of his kith and kin to say "I am the Lord's."

Frequently when converts come to cast in their lot with us they will say, "I do not know one in all my family who makes any profession of godliness: they are all of them opposed to me." In such a case the soul is among lions, and it is very hard and trying to be in such a position. Well may we pity a godly wife bound to an ungodly husband. Alas! full often a drunkard, whose opposition amounts to brutality. A tender, loving spirit, that ought to have been cherished like a tender flower, is bruised and trodden under foot, and made to suffer till the heart cries out in grief, "My soul is among lions." We little know what life-long martyrdoms many pious women endure. Children also have to bear the same when they are singled out by divine grace from depraved and wicked families.

Only the other day there came under my notice one who loves the Lord. I thought that if she had been a daughter of mine I should have rejoiced beyond all things in her sweet and gentle piety, but the parent said, "You must leave our house if you attend such-and-such a place of worship. We do not believe in these things, and we cannot have you about us if you do." I saw the grief which that state of things was causing, and though I could not alter it I mourned over it. Woe unto those who tyrannize over my Lord's little ones.

Nobody knows what godly working men have to put up with from those among whom they labour. There are some shops where there is religious liberty; but frequently the working men of this city are great tyrants in matters of religion. I tell them that to their faces. If a man will drink with them, and swear with them, they will make him their companion; but when a man comes out to fear God they make it very hard for him. And pray, sir, has not a man as much right to pray as you have to swear? And has he not as much right to believe in God as you have to disbelieve? It is a wonderfully free country, this! A wonderfully free country! A true Briton gives that liberty to others which he claims for himself, and if he does not choose to be religious himself he stands up like a man to defend the rights of others to be so if they choose. Now, then, ye British workmen, when shall we see you doing this?

The text speaks of a soul among lions. Why did the psalmist call them lions? "Dogs" is about as good a name as they deserve.

Why call them lions? Because at times the Christian man is exposed to enemies who are very strong—perhaps strong in the jaw—very strong in biting, rending, and tearing. Sometimes the Christian man is exposed to those who loudly roar out their infidelities and their blasphemies against Christ, and it is an awful thing to be among such lions as those. The lion is not only strong but cruel; and it is real cruelty which subjects well-meaning men to reproach and misrepresentation. The enemies of Christ and His people are often as cruel as lions, and would slay *us* if the law permitted them.

The lion is a creature of great craftiness, creeping along stealthily, and then making a sudden spring; and so will the ungodly creep up to the Christian, and, if possible, spring upon him when they can catch him in an unguarded moment. If they fancy they spy a fault in him they come down upon him with all their weight! The ungodly watch the righteous, and if they can catch them in their speech, or if they can make them angry, and cause them to speak an unguarded word, how eagerly they pounce upon him. They magnify his fault, put it under a microscope of ten thousand power, and make a great thing of it. "Report it! Report it!" they say. "So would we have it!" Anything against a true-born child of God is a sweet nut for them. Such as are daily watched, daily carped at, daily abused, daily hindered in everything that is good and gracious, go with their tears before the God they serve and cry to Him, "My soul is among lions."

Now, it is to such that I am going to speak to-night, a little at first *by way of comfort,* and then a little *by way of advice.*

I. First, BY WAY OF COMFORT. You are among lions, my dear young friend, then *you will have fellowship with your Lord and with His church.* Every Lord's-day, and every time we meet, this benediction is pronounced upon you, that you may enjoy the fellowship of the Holy Ghost. Fellowship with the Holy Ghost brings you into fellowship with Jesus, and this involves your being conformed to His sufferings. Now, your Lord was among lions. The men of His day had not a good word to say for Him. They called the Master of the house Beelzebub, they will never call you a worse name than that. They said that He was a drunken man and a wine-bibber; possibly they may say much the same as that of you, and it will be equally false. You need not be ashamed to be pelted with the same dirt that was thrown at your Master; and if it should ever come to this, that you should be stripped of everything, and false witness should rise up against you, and you should even be condemned as a felon, and taken out to execution, still your lot will not be worse than His.

Remember that you are the followers of a Crucified Lord, and cannot expect to be the world's darlings. If you are Christians, the inspired description of the Christian life is the taking up of the cross. Do you expect to be dandled on the knees of that same ungodly world which hung your Master upon the gibbet? No; you know that he who is the friend of this world is the enemy of God. This truth is unchangeable. It is just as certain to-day as it was in years gone by, that "the evil hateth the righteous, and gnasheth upon him with his teeth." You may pick up a fashionable religion, and get through the world with it very comfortably; but if you have the true faith you will have to fight for it. If you are of the world, the world will love its own; but if you are not of the world, because the Lord has chosen you out of the world, the world will hate you.

Nor was your Master alone. Recollect the long line of prophets that went before Christ. Which of them was it that was received with honour? Did they not stone one and slay another with the sword, cut one in pieces with a saw, put others to death with stones? Ye know that the march of the faithful may be tracked by their blood. And after our Lord had gone to heaven, how did the world treat the church? In the streets of Rome, and all large cities, the fierce cry was often heard, "Christians to the lions! Christians to the lions! Christians to the lions!" At dead of night men cry "Fire!" when a house is blazing; or a mob will cry "Bread!" when they are starving; but *the* cry of old Rome that was dearest to the Roman heart, and most expressive of their horrible enmity to goodness, was "Christians to the lions!"

Of all the gallant shows the Roman Empire ever saw, that which excited the populace beyond all things else was to see a family—a man and his wife, perhaps, and a grown-up daughter and son, and three or four children—all marched into the arena, and the big door thrown up, that out might rush the lion and spring upon them, and tear them to pieces. What harm had they done? They had forgiven their enemies. That was one of their great sins. They would not worship the gods of wood and stone. They would not blaspheme the name of Jesus whom they loved, for He had taught them to love one another, and to love all mankind. For such things as this men raised the cry, "Christians to the lions! Christians to the lions!" All along this has been the cry of the world against all who have faithfully followed in the steps of Jesus Christ. Just now the merciful hand of providence prevents open persecution, but only let that hand be taken away, and the old spirit will rage again. The seed of the serpent hates the seed of the woman still; and if the old dragon were not chained he would devour the man-child, as he has often tried to do. Do not deceive yourselves, in one form or other the old howl of "Christians to the lions!" would soon be heard in London if almighty power did not sit upon the throne and restrain the wrath of man.

You who have to suffer a measure of persecution for Christ's sake ought to be very glad of it, for you are counted worthy not only to be Christians, but to suffer for Christ's sake. Do not, I pray you, be unworthy of your high calling, but endure hardness as good soldiers of Jesus Christ. In these afflictions you are having fellowship with your Head and with His mystical body, therefore be not ashamed.

Here is another thought. If you are among lions *you should thereby be driven nearer to your God.* When you had a great many friends you could rejoice in them; but now that these turn against you, and the truth has come home to you—"A man's foes shall be they of his own household,"—what ought you to do? Why, get closer to God than ever you were before. Jesus Christ so loved His church that He said as He looked at His poor disciples, "These are my mother, and sister, and brother." You should do what your Master did—make His church your father and mother and sister and brother; nay, better still, make Christ all these to you and more. Take the Lord Jesus to be everything that all the dearest of mortals could be and far more. Sing that charming verse, which is a great favourite of mine, for it was very precious to me in days gone by—

> "If on my face, for Thy dear name,
>   Shame and reproaches be,
> All hail reproach, and welcome shame,
>   If Thou remember me."

Be sure that you live near to God. All Christians ought to do so, but you especially should be driven by every false accusation, by every caustic remark, by every cutting sentence, nearer to your Father's bosom. The more they rebuke you the more constantly should you abide under the covert of His sacred wings, and find your joy in the Lord.

And, getting close to Christ, let me say to you now by way of advice, and by way of comfort too, *endeavour to be very calm and happy.* Do not mind it. Take as little notice of the scoff as ever you can. It is a grand thing to have one deaf ear. Mind that you keep yourself very deaf to slander and reproach, as the psalmist did when he said, "I was as a man that heareth not, and in whose mouth are no reproofs." One blind eye towards the folly of enemies is often of more use to a man than two that are always looking about with suspicion. Do not see everything, do not hear everything. When there is a hard word spoken, do not notice it; or if you must hear it, forget it as quickly as ever you can. Love others all the more the less they love you: repay their enmity with love. Heap coals of fire upon them by making no return to a hard speech except by another deed of kindness. Very seldom defend yourself: it is a waste of breath, and casting pearls before swine. Bear and bear again.

Recollect that our Lord has sent us forth as sheep among wolves, and sheep cannot defend themselves. The wolf can eat all the sheep if it likes; but, do you not see, there are more *sheep* in the world now than there were wolves, ten thousand to one? Though the wolves have had all the eating, and though there never yet was a sheep that devoured a wolf, yet still the sheep are here and the wolves have gone. The sheep have won that victory: and so will Christ's little flock. The anvil is struck by the hammer, and the anvil never strikes in return, and yet the anvil wears the hammer out. Patience baffles fury and vanquishes malice. The non-resistance principle involves a resistance which is irresistible. The steady patience that cannot be provoked, but which, like Jesus, when reviled reviles not again, is certain of conquest. This is what you persecuted ones need to learn—to get more near your God the more you are among the lions, and so to be the more calm and patient the more men rage against you.

A third piece of comfort is this. Please to recollect that, although your soul is among lions, *the lions are chained*. When Daniel was thrown into the lions' den the lions were hungry and would soon have devoured him; but you know why it was that they could not touch him. Ah, the angel came. Just as the fierce lions were about to seize on Daniel, down he came swift from heaven, and stood in front of them. "Hush!" said he, and they lay as still as a stone. So says the text: "My God hath sent his angel and shut the lions' mouths." They had fine teeth, but their mouths were shut. If the Lord can easily shut a lion's mouth, He can quite as easily shut the mouth of an ungodly man. He can take off all trouble from you, if He wills it, in an instant, and He can give you a smooth path to heaven when it pleases Him; only remember that if everything on the road to heaven were smooth, heaven would not be so sweet at the end, and we should not have an opportunity of displaying those Christian graces which are brought out and educated by the opposition of the world.

God will not quench the fire of persecution, for it consumes our dross, but He will moderate its power so that not a grain of pure metal shall be lost. The lions are chained, dear friend; they can go no farther than God permits. In this country the most they can do, as a rule, is to howl, they cannot bite; and howling does not break bones; why, then, be afraid? The man who is afraid of being laughed at is not half a man, but almost deserves the scorn he receives. Never mind what is said. Talking will not hurt you. Harden your spirit against it, and bear it gallantly. Go and tell your Lord of it if your heart fails you; and then go forward, calm as your Master was, fearing nothing, for God will bear you through. The lions can roar, but they cannot rend—fear them not.

Another fact for your comfort is this; *when your soul is among lions, there is another lion there* as well as the lions that you can see. Have you never heard of Him? He is the Lion of the tribe of Judah. How quietly He lies! How patiently He waits by the side of His servants! The jest, the jeer, the noise continue, and He lies still. If He only would—if He thought it wise, if it were not for His superlative patience—He has only to rouse Himself for one moment, and all our enemies would be destroyed. Our great Lord and King could have had twelve legions of angels when He was in the garden for the lifting of His finger, but He continued a lone, a suffering man. If He willed it at this day He could sweep the ungodly away as chaff before the wind: His longsuffering is for their salvation, if haply they may turn and repent. If your faith be as it should be, it will be a great joy to you to know that He is always with you, that He is always near you. If He is ever absent from others of His servants, He is never away from His persecuted servants.

Ask the Covenanters amongst the mosses and the hills, and they will tell you that they never had such Sabbaths in Scotland as when they met among the crags, and set their scouts to warn them against Claverhouse's dragoons. When Cargill or Cameron thundered out the word, with what power was it attended. How sweetly was the blessed Bridegroom with His persecuted church among the hills. There is never such a time for seeing the Son of God as when the world heats the furnace seven times hotter. There is the flaming furnace, go and stand at the mouth of it and look in. They threw three men bound into it in their hosen and in their hats, and the flame was so strong that it killed the soldiers who threw them in. But look! Can you not see? Nebuchadnezzar himself comes to look. See how greatly he is astonished! He calls to those around him, and he demands, "Did not we cast three men bound into the furnace? Look ye, there are four. A strange, mysterious form is that fourth. They are walking the coals as if they walked in a garden of flowers. They seem full of delight, they are walking calmly as men converse in their gardens in the cool of the day; and that fourth—that mysterious fourth—is like the Son of God!"

Ah, Nebuchadnezzar, thou hast seen a sight that has often

been seen elsewhere. When God's people are in the furnace, God's Son is in the furnace also. He will not leave those who will not leave Him. If we can cling to Him, rest assured that He will cling to us, even to the end. Fear not the lions, then. Our Samson would turn upon them, and rend them in a moment if their hour were come.

> "Jesu's tremendous name
> Puts all our foes to flight;
> Jesus, the meek, the angry Lamb,
> A Lion is in fight.

> "By all hell's host withstood,
> We all hell's host o'erthrow;
> And conquering them, through Jesu's blood
> We still to conquer go."

Again, I want to comfort you with this word: you whose souls are among lions should recollect that *you will come out of the lions' den unharmed.* Daniel was cast into the den. Darius could not sleep that night, and when he went in in the morning he did not expect to find a bone of Daniel left, and so he began crying out to him. How surprised he must have been when Daniel replied that his God had preserved him. How thankful he was to fetch him out of the den. You, too, dear child of God, will come out of the den all right. There will be a resurrection of God's people's bodies at last, and there will be a resurrection for their reputations also. The slanderer may belie the character of a true man, but no true man's character will ever be buried long enough to rot. Your righteousness shall come forth as light, and your judgment as the noonday. You need not be afraid but that, as Daniel rose from the den to dignity, so will every man who suffers for Christ receive honour and glory and immortality "in that day."

Recollect that if you are among the lions now, *the day is hurrying on with speed when you shall be among the angels.* Our Lord and Master, after being in the wilderness with the wild beasts, found that "angels came and ministered to him." Such a visitation awaits all the faithful. What a change those martyrs enjoyed who took a fiery breakfast on earth, but supped with Christ that very day after riding to glory in a chariot of fire. If you have now to suffer all that can possibly be wreaked of vengeance upon you for Christ's sake, you will think nothing of it when you have been five minutes in heaven. Indeed, it will be a subject of congratulation that ever you were permitted in your humble measure to be counted worthy to suffer for Christ's sake. Therefore, be ye comforted, you young people, and march on with heroic step.

I see a soldier or two here to-night, and I am right glad that we have generally a block of them in the congregation. I know that often in the barrack-room it is hard for a Christian man to bear witness for Jesus Christ. Many and many a soldier has found his path as a Christian to be extremely difficult; he has had to sail very carefully, like a ship among torpedoes, and only divine grace has kept him safe. Some of you who reside in large establishments, where you sleep in rooms with a great many others, find it difficult even to kneel down to pray. Mind that you do it, though. Do it at first right bravely, and keep it up. Never be ashamed of your colours. Begin as you mean to go on; and go on as you begin. If you begin parleying you will soon lose all their respect, and make it worse for yourself; but in the name of Jesus Christ let me beseech you to be firm and steadfast even unto death. Be comforted, for there has no new thing happened to you. It is no novelty for the followers of Jesus to be ridiculed and despised. He came to send fire on the earth, and it has been kindled wellnigh two thousand years. The fiery path is the old road of the church militant; therefore tread it, and be glad that you are permitted to follow the heroes of heaven in their sacred way.

II. Now, a few words BY WAY OF ADVICE.

Of course this does not deal with all of you who are now present—I hope that many of you dwell among the godly. Still there are some whose soul is among lions, and to them I give this counsel.

First, if you dwell among lions *do not irritate them.* If I happened to be among lions I would not tease them: I would take good care that if they were cruel and fierce I did not make them so. I have known some, who I hope were Christians, who have acted very unwisely, and so have made matters bad for themselves. There is such a thing as ramming religion down people's throats, or trying to do so; and you can put on a very long face, and try to scold people into religion. This will not do. Never yet was anybody bullied to Christ, and there never will be. Some are very stern, and make no allowances for other people: these may be good, but they are not wise. What is a rule to you and to me may not be a rule to everybody else. We said the other Sunday that we should not think of eating what we give to swine; but we do not, therefore, say, "These swine must not have their wash." No, no; it is good enough for them. Let them have it. And as to worldly people and their amusements, let them have them, poor things. They have nothing else, let them have their mirth. I would not touch their joys, nor would you, for they would be no pleasure to you; but do not, as a new-born man, go and set yourself up as the standard of what the ordinary sinner, dead in sin, is to be. He cannot come up to our standard. Do not be perpetually finding fault: that is pulling the lions' whiskers, and the creatures are very likely to growl at you. If your soul is among lions, be gentle, be kind, be prudent, be tender. Sometimes be silent: a good word is on your tongue, but there are times when you must not say it: for the life of you, you must not say it, for it would rouse the lions and make more sin than need be.

Sometimes a truth needs defending; but, my inexperienced and untaught brother, do not try to defend it, for you have not the strength. The champion of infidelity will challenge one who is weak and uninstructed, and he overthrows him, and he who came forth valorously is beaten in argument. He was not up to the mark in knowledge, and so he was vanquished: and then, what do the adversaries say? Why, they boast that the truth is disproved and that Christ is beaten. Nothing of the kind. The British empire was not defeated when a regiment of our soldiers were slain at Isandula; and the truth and cause of Christ is not defeated when some weak champion full of zeal rushes to the front when he ought to have kept in the rear.

Secondly, if your soul is among lions, *do not roar yourself*, for that is very easy to be done. We have known some, who we hope were Christians, who have met railing with railing, hard words with hard words, bitter speeches with bitter speeches. The ungodly are lions, and you are not; do not try to meet them in their own line. You will never roar as well as they do. If you are a Christian man, you have not the knack of roaring. Leave *them* to do it. Your way of meeting them is not by losing your temper and abusing your antagonists, and so becoming a lion yourself; but you must conquer them with gentleness, patience, kindness, love. I pray you, dear brothers and sisters who have to bear a good deal for Christ's sake, do not get soured in spirit. There is a tendency in a martyr age to become obstinate and pugnacious. You must not be so. Love, love, love; and the more you are provoked, love the more. Overcome evil with good. I think it necessary to mention these cautions, because I know many require them.

Again, your soul is among lions: then, *do not be cowardly*. Have you never heard that a lion is afraid of a man if he looks him steadily in the face? I am not sure about that piece of natural history; but I am quite certain that it is true with regard to the ungodly world. If a man will bear himself calmly—if he will be unmoved, determined, resolute, steadfast—he will overcome the adversary. "When a man's ways please the Lord he maketh even his enemies to be at peace with him." If you give way a little, you will have to give way a great deal. If you give the world an inch, you will have to give it an ell, as sure as you are alive. If you will not yield an inch, nay, nor yet a barley-corn, but stand steadfast, God will help you. Courage is what is wanted.

> "Stand up! stand up for Jesus!
> The fight will not be long;
> This day the noise of battle,
> The next the victor's song."

Even if the fight were long, for such a Master as Jesus it were worth while to endure ten thousand years of scorn, and moreover the reward at the end will repay us a thousandfold.

If your soul is among lions, then *do not go out among them alone.* "Then whom shall I take with me?" says one, "there is not a Christian in the shop." Take your Lord with you. Be sure that you do that. Now, my dear friend, I know what they said yesterday, and how they bantered you; and you were tart and short with them, because you had not been in prayer in the morning as you ought to have been. If your mind had been more calm and gentle as the result of prayer you would not have mingled it one-half so much. Take your Master with you, and whenever you have to speak think that He is standing at your side, and try to say what you would like Him to hear; and then, when you have made your defence you will be able to say, "Good Master, I think I have not dishonoured thee, for I have spoken thy words." Oh, live near to Christ if you live among lions. Those of you who endure opposition make the best Christians. Many that have been distinguished for Christ in after life have had to rough it a little at first. "It is good for a man that he bear the yoke in his youth." If I could bring a garden-roller and roll the grass for you all the way from here to heaven do you think that I would do it? Certainly not. A rough place or two is good for you, it tries and strengthens pilgrim feet. A child will never become a man if he is carried about all his life like a baby. You must run alone. You must learn the arts of holy warfare, or else you will not be fit to be a soldier of the cross, a follower of the Lamb. May His good Spirit help you to keep in fellowship with Christ, that He may guard and protect you from every temptation and persecution.

Further, let me say to you that if your soul is among lions, and you feel very weak about it, you are permitted to *pray the Lord to move you in His providence to quieter quarters.* A Christian man is not bound to endure persecution if he can help it. "When they persecute you in one city flee to another." You are quite warranted in seeking another situation. There may be reasons why you should remain under the trial, and if so, take care that you do not overlook them. Prudence may make you avoid persecution, but cowardice must not mingle with the prudence. That prayer which says, "Lead us not into temptation," gives us, as it were, a permit to remove from places where we are much tempted; and sometimes it is the duty of the Christian to seek some other sphere of labour, if he possibly can, where he will not be so much tried.

One thought more: *the braver thing is to ask for grace to stop with the lions and tame them.* "My soul is among lions." Well, if the Lord makes you a lion tamer, that is the very place where you ought to be. In some of our districts in London as soon as ever a man is converted he feels that he cannot live there any longer, and this makes the district hopeless. Sometimes the Christian man should say, "No: God has made me strong in grace; and I will stop here, and fight it out. These are lions, but I will tame them. I believe that God has put me here on purpose to bring my fellow-workmen to the Saviour, and by His grace I will do it."

And now, Christian people, is there not sense about this advice? Is there not reason in it? Would not your Master have you go where you are most wanted, and should you not, therefore, if your soul is amongst lions, say, "Thank God it is so. These people are not going to conquer me, but I am going to conquer them"?

What a beautiful spectacle was that which was exhibited by the Moravian Brethren in their grand times! They could not land on one of the West Indies to preach the gospel to the negroes, for the planters would not have anybody there but slaves; and two brethren sold themselves for slaves, and lived and died in bondage, that they might teach the poor negroes. It is said that there was a place in Africa where persons were shut up whose limbs were rotting away through leprosy and other diseases. Two of these brethren climbed up the wall and saw these poor creatures—some with no legs, and others with no arms. They asked to be allowed to go in to win their souls for Christ, and the answer was, "If you enter you can never come out again, because you would bring contagion. You go in there to die, to rot away as the lepers do." These brave men went in and died that they might bring the lepers to Christ. I hope that we have some drops of that grand Christian blood still in our veins; and if we have, we shall feel that we could go to the gates of hell to win a sinner.

You are not like your Master unless you would die to save men from hell. You will bear jests and jeers, and count them nothing if you can but win souls. So stop where you are, my stronger brothers and sisters; if your souls are among lions, tarry and tame the lions. It will be a grand thing for you to come one day to the church-meeting with two or three of your neighbours whom you have been the means of converting to Christ. I like to see a man march, if he can do it, with a tame lion on each side. When a man has by God's grace brought some of those that were drunkards and swearers to the feet of Jesus, oh, it is a grand triumph. It has been my business for many years to be a lion tamer, and I delight in it. If there is any lion of the sort here, I wish the Master would tame him, and make him lie down and crouch at His feet. There is the place for us poor sinners, at the feet of Christ. But do not be afraid of sinners, dear friends, for how can you tame them if you tremble at them. Go forth to win them in the strength of the living God, and you shall yet see the lion lie down with the lamb, and a little child shall lead them. Amen and amen.

THE TALKING BOOK

A Sermon

Text.—"When thou awakest, it shall talk with thee."—Proverbs vi. 22.

It is a very happy circumstance when the commandment of our father and the law of our mother are also the commandment of God and the law of the Lord. Happy are they who have a double force to draw them to the right—the bonds of nature, and the cords of grace. They sin with a vengeance who sin both against a father on earth and the great Father in heaven, and they exhibit a virulence and a violence of sin who do despite to the tender obligations of childhood, as well as to the demands of conscience and God. Solomon, in the passage before us, evidently speaks of those who find in the parents' law and in God's law the same thing, and he admonishes such to bind the law of God about their heart, and to tie it about their neck; by which he intends inward affection and open avowal.

No blush is to mantle our cheek when we are called Christians; we are never to speak with bated breath in any company concerning the things of God. Manfully must we take up the cross of Christ; cheerfully must we avow ourselves to belong to those who have respect unto the divine testimonies. Let us count true religion to be our highest ornament; and, as magistrates put upon them their gold chains, and think themselves adorned thereby, so let us tie about our neck the commands and the gospel of the Lord our God.

In order that we may be persuaded so to do, Solomon gives us three telling reasons. He says that God's law, by which I understand the whole run of Scripture, and, especially the gospel of Jesus Christ, will be a guide to us:—"When thou goest, it shall lead thee." It will be a guardian to us: "When thou sleepest"—when thou art defenceless and off thy guard—"it shall keep thee." And it shall also be a dear companion to us: "When thou awakest, it shall talk with thee." Any one of these three arguments might surely suffice to make us seek a nearer acquaintance with the sacred word.

But I prefer, this morning, to keep to the third reason for loving God's word. It is this, that it becomes *our sweet companion :* "When thou awakest, it shall talk with thee." The inspired law of God, which David in the hundred and nineteenth Psalm calls God's testimonies, precepts, statutes, and the like, is the

friend of the righteous. Its essence and marrow is the gospel
of Jesus, the law-fulfiller, and this also is the special solace of
believers. Of the whole sacred volume it may be said, "When
thou awakest, it shall talk with thee." I gather four or five
thoughts from this expression, and upon these we will speak.

I. We perceive here that THE WORD IS LIVING. How else could
it be said: "It shall talk with thee"? A dead book cannot talk,
nor can a dumb book speak. It is clearly a living book, then,
and a speaking book: "The word of God, which liveth and
abideth for ever." How many of us have found this to be most
certainly true! A large proportion of human books are long ago
dead, and even shrivelled like Egyptian mummies; the mere
course of years has rendered them worthless, their teaching is
disproved, and they have no life for us. Entomb them in your
public libraries if you will, but, henceforth, they will stir no
man's pulse and warm no man's heart. But this thrice blessed
book of God, though it has been extant among us these many
hundreds of years, is immortal in its life, unwithering in its
strength: the dew of its youth is still upon it; its speech still
drops as the rain fresh from heaven; its truths are overflowing
founts of ever fresh consolation. Never book spake like this
book; its voice, like the voice of God, is powerful and full of
majesty.

Whence comes it that the word of God is living? Is it not,
first, because *it is pure truth* ? Error is death, truth is life. No
matter how well established an error may be by philosophy, or
by force of arms, or the current of human thought, the day
cometh that shall burn as an oven, and all untruth shall be as
stubble before the fire. The tooth of time devours all lies.
Falsehoods are soon cut down, and they wither as the green
herb. Truth never dies, it dates its origin from the immortals.
Kindled at the source of light, its flame cannot be quenched;
if by persecution it be for a time covered, it shall blaze forth
anew to take reprisals upon its adversaries. Many a once
venerated system of error now rots in the dead past among
the tombs of the forgotten; but the truth as it is in Jesus knows
no sepulchre, and fears no funeral; it lives on, and must live
while the Eternal fills His throne.

The word of God is living, because *it is the utterance of an im-
mutable, self-existing God*. God doth not speak to-day what He
meant not yesterday, neither will He to-morrow blot out what
He records to-day. When I read a promise spoken three thousand
years ago, it is as fresh as though it fell from the eternal lips
to-day. There are, indeed, no dates to the Divine promises;
they are not of private interpretation, nor to be monopolised
by any generation. I say again, as fresh to-day the eternal

word drops from the Almighty's lips as when He uttered it to Moses, or to Elias, or spake it by the tongue of Esaias or Jeremiah. The word is always sure, steadfast, and full of power. It is never out of date. Scripture bubbles up evermore with good matters, it is an eternal Geyser, a spiritual Niagara of grace, for ever falling, flashing, and flowing on; it is never stagnant, never brackish or defiled, but always clear, crystal, fresh, and refreshing; so, therefore, ever living.

The word lives, again, because *it enshrines the living heart of Christ*. The heart of Christ is the most living of all existences. It was once pierced with a spear, but it lives on, and yearns towards sinners, and is as tender and compassionate as in the days of the Redeemer's flesh. Jesus, the Sinner's Friend, walks in the avenues of Scripture as once He traversed the plains and hills of Palestine: you can see Him still, if you have opened eyes, in the ancient prophecies; you can behold Him more clearly in the devout evangelists; He opens and lays bare His inmost soul to you in the epistles, and makes you hear the footsteps of His approaching advent in the symbols of the Apocalypse. The living Christ is in the book; you behold His face almost in every page; and, consequently, it is a book that can talk. The Christ of the mount of benedictions speaks in it still; the God who said, "Let there be light," gives forth from its pages the same divine fiat; while the incorruptible truth, which saturated every line and syllable of it when first it was penned, abides therein in full force, and preserves it from the finger of decay. "The grass withereth, and the flower thereof falleth away: but the word of the Lord endureth for ever."

Over and above all this, *the Holy Spirit has a peculiar connection with the word of God*. I know that He works in the ministries of all His servants whom He hath ordained to preach; but for the most part, I have remarked that the work of the Spirit of God in men's hearts is rather in connection with the texts we quote than with our explanations of them. "Depend upon it," says a deeply spiritual writer, "it is God's word, not man's comment on it, which saves souls." God does save souls by our comment, but still it is true that the majority of conversions have been wrought by the agency of a text of Scripture. It is the word of God that is living, and powerful, and sharper than any two-edged sword. There must be life in it, for by it men are born again. As for believers, the Holy Spirit often sets the word on a blaze while they are studying it. The letters were at one time before us as mere letters, but the Holy Ghost suddenly came upon them, and they spake with tongues. The chapter is lowly as the bush at Horeb, but the Spirit descends upon it, and lo! it glows with celestial splendour, God appearing in the words, so that we feel like Moses when he put off his shoes from his feet, because the place whereon he stood was holy ground.

It is true, the mass of readers understand not this, and look upon the Bible as a common book; but if they understand it not, as least let them allow the truthfulness of our assertion, when we declare that hundreds of times we have as surely felt the presence of God in the page of Scripture as ever Elijah did when he heard the Lord speaking in a still small voice. The Bible has often appeared to us as a temple God, and the posts of its doors have moved at the voice of Him that cried, whose train also has filled the temple. We have been constrained adoringly to cry, with the seraphim, "Holy, holy, holy, is the Lord God of Hosts." God the Holy Spirit vivifies the letter with His presence, and then it is to us a living word indeed.

And now, dear brethren, if these things be so—and our experience certifies them—let us take care how we trifle with a book which is so instinct with life. Might not many of you remember your faults this day were we to ask you whether you are habitual students of holy writ? Readers of it I believe you are; but are you searchers; for the promise is not to those who merely read, but to those who delight in the law of the Lord, and meditate therein both day and night. Are you sitting at the feet of Jesus, with His word as your school-book? If not, remember, though you may be saved, you lack very much of the blessing which otherwise you might enjoy. Have you been backsliding? Refresh your soul by meditating in the divine statutes, and you will say, with David, "Thy word hath quickened me." Are you faint and weary? Go and talk with this living book: it will give you back your energy, and you shall mount again as with the wings of eagles.

But are you unconverted altogether? Then I cannot direct you to Bible-reading as being the way of salvation, nor speak of it as though it had any merit in it; but I would, nevertheless, urge upon you unconverted people great reverence for Scripture, an intimate acquaintance with its contents, and a frequent perusal of its pages, for it has occurred ten thousand times over that when men have been studying the word of life, the word has brought life to them. "The entrance of thy word giveth light." Like Elijah and the dead child, the word has stretched itself upon them, and their dead souls have been made to live. One of the likeliest places in which to find Christ is in the garden of the Scriptures, for there He delights to walk. As of old, the blind men were wont to sit by the wayside begging, so that, if Jesus passed by, they might cry to Him, so would I have you sit down by the wayside of the Holy Scriptures. Hear the promises, listen to their gracious words; they are the footsteps of the Saviour; and, as you hear them, may you be led to cry, "Thou Son of David, have mercy upon me!" "Faith cometh by hearing, and hearing by the word of God."

II. If the text says, "When thou awakest, it shall talk with thee," then it is clear THE WORD IS PERSONAL. "It shall talk with *thee*." It is not written, "It shall speak to the air, and thou shalt hear its voice," but, "It shall talk with *thee*," that is to say, *God's word talks about men, and about modern men*; it speaks of ourselves, and of these latter days, as precisely as if it had only appeared this last week. Some go to the word of God with the idea that they shall find historical information about the ancient ages, and so they will, but that is not the object of the Word. Others look for facts upon geology, and great attempts have been made either to bring geology round to Scripture, or Scripture to geology. We may always rest assured that truth never contradicts itself; but the main teachings of Holy Scripture are about men, about the Paradise of unfallen manhood, the fall, the degeneracy of the race, and the means of its redemption. The book speaks of victims and sacrifices, priests and washings, and so points us to the divine plan by which man can be elevated from the fall and be reconciled to God. Read Scripture through, and you shall find that its great subject is that which concerns the race as to their most important interests. It is a book that talks, talks personally, for it deals with things not in the moon, nor in the planet Jupiter, nor in the distant ages long gone by, nor does it say much of the periods yet to come, but it deals with *us*, with the business of to-day; how sin may be to-day forgiven, and our souls brought at once into union with Christ.

Moreover, this book is so personal, that *it speaks to men in all states and conditions before God*. How it talks to sinners—talks, I say, for its puts it thus: "Come, now, and let us reason together; though your sins be as scarlet, they shall be as wool; though they be red like crimson, they shall be as snow." It has many very tender expostulations for sinners. It stoops to their condition and position. If they will not stoop to God, it makes, as it were, eternal mercy stoop to them. It talks of feasts of fat things, of fat things full of marrow; and the book, as it talks, reasons with men's hunger, and bids them eat and be satisfied. In all conditions into which the sinner can be cast, there is a word that precisely meets his condition.

And, certainly, when we become the children of God the book talks with us wondrously. In the family of heaven it is the child's own book. We no sooner know our Father than this dear book comes at once as a love letter from the far-off country, signed with our own Father's hand, and perfumed with our Father's love. If we grow in grace, or if we backslide, in either case Scripture still talks with us. Whatever our position before the eternal God, the book seems to be written on purpose to meet that position. It talks to you as you are, not only as you should be, or as others have been, but with you, with you personally, about your present condition.

Have you never noticed how personal the book is as *to all your states of mind*, in reference to sadness or to joy? There was a time with some of us when we were very gloomy and sore depressed, and then the book of Job mourned to the same dolorous tune. I have turned over the Lamentations of Jeremiah, and thought that I could have written just what Jeremiah wrote. It mourns unto us when we lament.

On the other hand, when the soul gets up to the exceeding high mountains, to the top of Amana and Lebanon, when we behold visions of glory, and see our Beloved face to face, lo! the word is at our side, and in the delightful language of the Psalms, or in the yet sweeter expressions of the Song of Solomon, it tells us all that is in our heart, and talks to us as a living thing that has been in the deeps, and has been on the heights, that has known the overwhelmings of affliction, and has rejoiced in the triumphs of delight. The word of God is to me my own book: I have no doubt, brother, it is the same to you. There could not be a Bible that suited me better: it seems written on purpose for me. Dear sister, have not you often felt as you have put your finger on a promise, "Ah, that is my promise; if there be no other soul whose tearful eyes can bedew that page and say, 'It is mine,' yet I, a poor afflicted one, can do so!" Oh, yes; the book is very personal, for it goes into all the details of our case, let our state be what it may.

And, *how very faithful it always is*. You never find the word of God keeping back that which is profitable to you. Like Nathan it cries, "Thou art the man." It never allows our sins to go unrebuked, nor our backslidings to escape notice till they grow into overt sin. It gives us timely notice; it cries to us as soon as we begin to go aside, "Awake thou that sleepest," "Watch and pray," "Keep thine heart with all diligence," and a thousand other words of warning does it address personally to each one of us.

Now I would suggest, before I leave this point, a little self-examination as healthful for each of us. Does the word of God after this fashion speak to my soul? Then it is a gross folly to lose by generalisations that precious thing which can only be realised by a personal grasp. How sayest thou, dear hearer? dost thou read the book for thyself, and does the book speak to thee? Has it ever condemned thee, and hast thou trembled before the word of God? Has it ever pointed thee to Christ, and hast thou looked to Jesus the incarnate Saviour? Does the book now seal, as with the witness of the Spirit, the witness of thine own spirit that thou art born of God? Art thou in the habit of going to the book to know thine own condition, to see thine own face as in a glass? Is it thy family medicine? Is it thy test and tell-tale to let thee know thy spiritual condition? Oh, do not treat the book otherwise than this, for if thou dost thus unto it, and takest it to be thy personal friend, happy art thou, since God will dwell with the man that trembles at His word; but, if you treat it as anybody's book rather than your own, then beware, lest you be numbered with the wicked who despise God's statutes.

III. From the text we learn that HOLY SCRIPTURE IS VERY FAMILIAR. "When thou awakest, it shall *talk with* thee. To talk signifies fellowship, communion, familiarity. We sit at its feet, or rather at the feet of Jesus, in the Word, and it comes down to us; it is familiar with us, as a man talketh to his friend. And here let me remind you of the delightful familiarity of Scripture in this respect, that *it speaks the language of men.* If God had written us a book in His own language, we could not have comprehended it, or what little we understood would have so alarmed us, that we should have besought that those words should not be spoken to us any more; but the Lord, in His Word, often uses language which, though it be infallibly true in its meaning, is not after the knowledge of God, but according to the manner of man. I mean this, that the word uses similes and analogies of which we may say that they speak humanly, and not according to the absolute truth as God Himself sees it. As men conversing with babes use their broken speech, so doth the condescending word. It is not written in the celestial tongue, but in the *patois* of this lowland country, condescending to men of low estate. It feeds us on bread broken down to our capacity, "food convenient for us." It speaks of God's arm, His hand, His finger, His wings, and even of His feathers. Now, all this is familiar picturing, to meet our childish capacities; for the Infinite One is not to be conceived of as though such similitudes were literal facts. It is an amazing instance of divine love, that He puts those things so that we may be helped to grasp sublime truths. Let us thank the Lord of the word for this.

How tenderly Scripture *comes down to simplicity.* Suppose the sacred volume had all been like the book of the prophet Ezekiel, small would have been its service to the generality of mankind. Imagine that the entire volume had been as mysterious as the

Book of Revelation: it might have been our duty to study it, but if its benefit depended upon our understanding it, we should have failed to attain it. But how simple are the gospels, how plain these words, "He that believeth and is baptised shall be saved"; how deliciously clear those parables about the lost piece of money, the lost sheep, and the prodigal son. Wherever the word touches upon vital points, it is as bright as a sunbeam. Mysteries there are, and profound doctrines, deeps where Leviathan can swim; but, where it has to do immediately with what concerns us for eternity, it is so plain that the babe in grace may safely wade in its refreshing streams. In the gospel narrative the wayfaring man, though a fool, need not err. It is familiar talk; it is God's great mind brought down to our littleness, that it may lift us up.

How familiar the book is too—I speak now as to my own feelings—*as to all that concerns us.* It talks about my flesh, and my corruptions, and my sins, as only one that knew me could speak. It talks of my trials in the wisest way; some, I dare not tell, it knows all about. It talks about my difficulties; some would sneer at them and laugh, but this book sympathises with them, knows my tremblings, and my fears, and my doubts, and all the storm that rages within the little world of my nature. The book has been through all my experience; somehow or other it maps it all out, and talks with me as if it were a fellow-pilgrim. Have you not often wondered at the human utterances of the divine word: it thunders like God and yet weeps like man. It seems impossible that anything should be too little for the word of God to notice, or too bitter, or even too sinful for that book to overlook. It touches humanity at all points. Everywhere it is a personal, familiar acquaintance, and seems to say to itself, "Shall I hide this thing from Abraham my friend?"

And, how often the book has *answered enquiries*! I have been amazed in times of difficulties to see how plain the oracle is. You have asked friends, and they could not advise you; but you have gone to your knees, and God has told you. You have questioned, and you have puzzled, and you have tried to elucidate the problem, and, lo! in the chapter read at morning prayer, or in a passage of Scripture that lay open before you, the direction has been given. Have we not seen a text, as it were, plume its wings, and fly from the word like a seraph, and touch our lips with a live altar coal? It lay like a slumbering angel amidst the beds of spices of the sacred word, but it received a divine mission, and brought consolation and instruction to your heart.

The word of God, then, talks with us in the sense of being familiar with us. Do we understand this? I will close this point by another word of application. Who, then, that finds God's word so dear and kind a friend would spurn or neglect it? If any of you have despised it, what shall I say to you? If it were a dreary book, written within and without with curses and lamentations, whose every letter flashed with declarations of vengeance, I might see some reason why we should not read it; but, O precious, priceless companion, dear friend of all my sorrows, making my bed in my sickness, the light of my darkness, and the joy of my soul, how can I forget thee—how can I forsake thee?

I have heard of one who said that the dust on some men's Bibles lay there so thick and long that you might write "*Damnation*" on it. I am afraid that such is the case with some of you. Mr. Rogers, of Dedham, on one occasion, after preaching about the preciousness of the Bible, took it away from the front of the pulpit, and, putting it down behind him, pictured God as saying, "You do not read the book: you do not care about it; I will take it back—you shall not be wearied with it any more." And then he portrayed the grief of wise men's hearts when they found the blessed revelation withdrawn from men; and how they would besiege the throne of grace, day and night, to ask it back. I am sure he spoke the truth. Though we too much neglect it, yet ought we to prize it beyond all price, for, if it were taken from us, we should have lost our kindest comforter in the hour of need. God grant us to love the Scriptures more!

IV. Fourthly, and with brevity, our text evidently shows that THE WORD IS RESPONSIVE. "When thou awakest, it shall talk *with* thee," not *to* thee. Now, talk with a man is not all on one side. To talk with a man needs answering talk from him. You have both of you something to say when you talk together. It is a conversation to which each one contributes his part. Now, Scripture is a marvellously conversational book; it talks, and makes men talk. It is ever ready to respond to us. Suppose you go to the Scriptures in a certain state of spiritual life: you must have noticed, I think, that the word answers to that state. If you are dark and gloomy, it will appear as though it had put itself in mourning, so that it might lament with you. When you are on the dunghill, there sits Scripture, with dust and ashes on its head, weeping side by side with you, and not upbraiding like Job's miserable comforters.

But suppose you come to the book with gleaming eyes of joy, you will hear it laugh; it will sing and play to you as with psaltery and harp, it will bring forth the high-sounding cymbals. Enter its goodly land in a happy state, and you shall go forth with joy and be led forth with peace, its mountains and its hills shall break before you into singing, and all the trees of the field shall clap their hands. As in water the face is reflected, so in the living stream of revealed truth a man sees his own image.

If you come to Holy Scripture with growth in grace, and with aspirations for yet higher attainments, the book grows with you, grows upon you. It is ever beyond you, and cheerily cries, "Higher yet; Excelsior!" Many books in my library are now behind and beneath me; I read them years ago, with considerable pleasure; I have read them since, with disappointment; I shall never read them again, for they are of no service to me. They were good in their way once, and so were the clothes I wore when I was ten years old; but I have outgrown them, I know more than these books know, and know wherein they are faulty. Nobody ever outgrows Scripture; the book widens and deepens with our years. It is true, it cannot really grow, for it is perfect; but it does so to our apprehension. The deeper you dig into Scripture, the more you find that it is a great abyss of truth. The beginner learns four or five points of orthodoxy, and says, "I understand the gospel, I have grasped all the Bible." Wait a bit, and when his soul grows and knows more of Christ, he will confess, "Thy commandment is exceeding broad, I have onmy begun to understand it."

There is one thing about God's word which shows its responsiveness to us, and that is when you reveal your heart to it, it reveals its heart to you. If, as you read the word, you say, "O blessed truth, thou art indeed realised in my experience; come thou still further into my heart. I give up my prejudices, I assign myself, like the wax, to be stamped with thy seal,"—when you do that, and open your heart to Scripture, Scripture will open its heart to you; for it has secrets which it does not tell to the casual reader, it has precious things of the everlasting hills which can only be discovered by miners who know how to dig and open the secret places, and penetrate great veins of everlasting riches. Give thyself up to the Bible, and the Bible will give itself up to thee. Be candid with it, and honest with thy soul, and the Scripture will take down its golden key, and open one door after another, and show to thy astonished gaze ingots of silver which thou couldst not weigh, and heaps of gold which thou couldst not measure. Happy is that man who, in talking with the Bible, tells it all his heart, and learns the secret of the Lord which is with them that fear Him.

And how, too, if you love the Bible and talk out your love to it, the Bible will love you! Its wisdom says, "I love them that love me." Embrace the word of God, and the word of God embraces you at once. When you prize its every letter, then it smiles upon you graciously, greets you with many welcomes, and treats you as an honoured guest. I am always sorry to be on bad terms with the Bible, for then I must be on bad terms with God. Whenever my creed does not square with God's word, I think it is time to mould my creed into another form. The teachings of God's word are infallible, and must be reverenced as such. Now, when you love it so well that you would not touch a single line of it, and prize it so much that you would even die for the defence of one of its truths, then, as it is dear to you, you will be dear to it, and it will grasp you and unfold itself to you as it does not to the world.

Dear brethren and sisters, I must leave this point, but it shall be with this remark—Do you talk to God? Does God talk to you? Does your heart go up to heaven, and does His Word come fresh from heaven to your soul? If not, you do not know the experience of the living child of God, and I can earnestly pray you may. May you this day be brought to see Christ Jesus in the word, to see a crucified Saviour there, and to put your trust in Him, and then, from this day forward, the word will echo to your heart—it will respond to your emotions.

V. Lastly, SCRIPTURE IS INFLUENTIAL. That I gather from the fact that Solomon says, "When thou wakest, it shall talk with thee"; and follows it up with the remark that it keeps man from the strange woman, and from other sins which he goes on to mention. When the word of God talks with us, it influences us. All talk influences more or less. I believe there is more done in this world for good or bad by talk than there is by preaching; indeed, the preacher preaches best when he talks; there is no oratory in the world that is equal to simple talk: it is the model of eloquence; and all your rhetorician's action and verbiage are so much rubbish. Now, this book, as it talks with us, influences us, and it does so in many ways.

It soothes our sorrows, and encourages us. Many a warrior has been ready to steal away from God's battle, but the word has laid its hand on him, and said, "Stand on thy feet, be not discouraged, be of good cheer, I will strengthen thee, I will help thee; yea, I will uphold thee with the right hand of my righteousness." Brave saints we have read of, but we little know how often they would have been arrant cowards only the good word came and strengthened them, and they went back to be stronger than lions and swifter than eagles.

While the book thus soothes and cheers, it has a wonderfully elevating power. Have you never felt it put fresh life-blood into you? You have thought, "How can I continue to live at such a dying rate as I have lived, something nobler must I

gain?'' Read that part of the word which tells of the agonies
of your Master, and you will feel—

> "Now for the love I bear His name,
> What was my gain I count my loss;
> My former pride I call my shame,
> And nail my glory to His cross."

Read of the glories of heaven which this book reveals, and you
will feel that you can run the race with quickened speed, because a crown so bright is glittering in your view. Nothing can
so lift a man above the gross considerations of carnal gain or
human applause as to have his soul saturated with the spirit
of truth. It elevates as well as cheers.

Then, too, how often it warns and restrains. I had gone to
the right or to the left if the law of the Lord had not said, "Let
thine eyes look right on, and let thine eyelids look straight before
thee."

This book's consecrated talk sanctifies and moulds the mind
into the image of Christ. You cannot expect to grow in grace
if you do not read the Scriptures. If you are not familiar with
the word, you cannot expect to become like Him that spake it.
Our experience is, as it were, the potter's wheel on which we
revolve; and the hand of God is in the Scriptures to mould us
after the fashion and image which He intends to bring us to.
Oh, be much with the holy word of God, and you will be holy.
Be much with the silly novels of the day, and the foolish trifles
of the hour, and you will degenerate into vapid wasters of your
time; but be much with the solid teaching of God's word, and
you will become solid and substantial men and women: drink
them in, and feed upon them, and they shall produce in you
a Christ-likeness, at which the world shall stand astonished.

Lastly, let the Scripture talk with you, and it will confirm
and settle you. The word, the simple, pure, infallible word
of God, we must live upon if we are to become strong against
error, and tenacious of truth.

The time is coming when we shall all fall asleep in death.
Oh, how blessed it will be to find when we awake that the word
of God will talk with us then, and remember its ancient friend-
ship. Then the promise which we loved before shall be fulfilled;
the charming intimations of a blessed future shall be all realised,
and the face of Christ, whom we saw as through a glass darkly,
shall be all uncovered, and He shall shine upon us as the sun
in its strength. God grant us to love the word, and feed thereon,
and the Lord shall have the glory for ever and ever. Amen
and amen.

PRODIGAL LOVE FOR THE PRODIGAL SON

A Sermon

Text.—"And kissed him."—Luke xv. 20.

In the Revised Version, if you will kindly look at the margin, you will find that the text there reads, "*And kissed him much.*" This is a very good translation of the Greek, which might bare the meaning, "Kissed him earnestly," or "Kissed him eagerly," or "Kissed him often." I prefer to have it in very plain language, and therefore adopt the marginal reading of the Revised Version, "Kissed him much," as the text of my sermon, the subject of which will be the overflowing love of God towards the returning sinner.

The first word "and" links us on to all that had gone before. The parable is a very familiar one, yet it is so full of sacred meaning that it always has some fresh lesson for us. Let us, then, consider the preliminaries to this kissing. On the son's side there was something, and on the father's side much more. Before the prodigal son received these kisses of love, he had said in the far country, "I will arise and go to my father." He had, however, done more than that, else his father's kiss would never have been upon his cheek. The resolve had become a deed: "He arose, and came to his father." A bushelful of resolutions is of small value; a single grain of practice is worth the whole. The determination to return home is good; but it is when the wandering boy begins the business of really carrying out the good resolve, that he draws near the blessing. If any of you here present have long been saying, "I will repent; I will turn to God," leave off resolving, and come to practising; and may God in His mercy lead you both to repent and to believe in Christ!

I do not suppose that the prodigal travelled very fast. I should imagine that he came very slowly—

> "With heavy heart and downcast eye,
> With many a sob and many a sigh."

He was resolved to come, yet he was half afraid. But we read that his father ran. Slow are the steps of repentance, but swift are the feet of forgiveness. God can run where we can scarcely limp, and if we are limping towards Him, He will run towards us.

These kisses were given in a hurry; the story is narrated in a way that almost makes us realise that such was the case: there is a sense of haste in the very wording of it. His father "ran, and fell on his neck, and kissed him"; —kissed him eagerly. He did not delay a moment; for though he was out of breath, he was not out of love. "He fell on his neck, and kissed him much." There stood his son ready to confess his sin; therefore did his father kiss him all the more.

The more willing thou art to own thy sin, the more willing is God to forgive thee. When thou dost make a clean breast of it, God will soon make a clear record of it. He will wipe out the sin that thou dost willingly acknowledge and humbly confess before Him. He that was willing to use his lips for confession, found that his father was willing to use his lips for kissing him.

See the contrast. There is the son, scarcely daring to think of embracing his father, yet his father has scarcely seen him before he has fallen on his neck. The condescension of God towards penitent sinners is very great. He seems to stoop from His throne of glory to fall upon the neck of a repentant sinner. God on the neck of a sinner! What a wonderful picture! Can you conceive it? I do not think you can; but if you cannot imagine it, I hope that you will realise it. When God's arm is about our neck, and His lips are on our cheek, kissing us much, then we understand more than preachers or books can ever tell us of His condescending love.

The father "saw" his son. There is a great deal in that word "saw." He saw who it was; saw where he had come from; saw the swineherd's dress; saw the filth upon his hands and feet; saw his rags; saw his penitent look; saw what he had been; saw what he was; and saw what he would soon be. "His father saw him." God has a way of seeing men and women that you and I cannot understand. He sees right through us at a glance, as if we were made of glass; He sees all our past, present and future.

"When he was yet a great way off, his father saw him." It was not with icy eyes that the father looked on his returning son. Love leaped into them, and as he beheld him, he "had compassion on him"; that is, he felt for him. There was no anger in his heart towards his son; he had nothing but pity for his poor boy, who had got into such a pitiable condition. It was true that it was all his own fault, but that did not come before his father's mind. It was the state that he was in, his poverty, his degradation, that pale face of his so wan with hunger, that touched his father to the quick. And God has compassion on the woes and miseries of men. They may have brought their troubles on themselves, and they have indeed done so; but nevertheless God has compassion upon them. "It is of the Lord's mercies that we are not consumed, because His compassions fail not."

We read that the father "ran." The compassion of God is followed by swift movements. He is slow to anger, but He is quick to bless. He does not take any time to consider how He shall show His love to penitent prodigals; that was all done long ago in the eternal covenant. He has no need to prepare for their return to Him; that was all done on Calvary. God comes flying in the greatness of His compassion to help every poor penitent soul.

> "On cherub and on cherubim,
>   Full royally He rode;
> And on the wings of mighty winds
>   Came flying all abroad."

And when He comes, He comes to kiss. "He fell on his neck, and kissed him"; kissed him eagerly, kissed him much.

What does this much kissing mean? It signifies that, when sinners come to God, He gives them a loving reception, and a hearty welcome. If any one of you, while I am speaking, shall come to God, expecting mercy because of the great sacrifice of Christ, this shall be true of you as it has been true of many of us: "He kissed him much."

I. First, this much kissing means MUCH LOVE. It means much love truly *felt*; for God never gives an expression of love without feeling it in His infinite heart. God will never give a Judas-kiss, and betray those whom He embraces. There is no hypocrisy with God; He never kisses those for whom He has no love. Oh, how God loves sinners! You who repent, and come to Him, will discover how greatly He loves you. There is no measuring the love He bears towards you. He has loved you from before the foundation of the world, and He will love you when time shall be no more. Oh, the immeasurable love of God to sinners who come and cast themselves upon His mercy!

This much kissing also means much love *manifested*. God's people do not always know the greatness of His love to them. Sometimes, however, it is shed abroad in our hearts by the Holy Ghost which is given unto us. Some of us know at times what it is to be almost too happy to live! The love of God has been so overpoweringly experienced by us on some occasions, that we have almost had to ask for a stay of the delight, because we could not endure any more. If the glory had not been veiled a little, we should have died of excess of rapture, or happiness. Beloved, God has wondrous ways of opening His people's hearts to the manifestation of His grace. He can pour in, not now and then a drop of His love, but great and mighty streams. Madame Guyon used to speak of the torrents of love that come sweeping through the spirit, bearing all before them. The poor prodigal in the parable had so much love manifested to him, that he might have sung of the torrents of his father's affection. That is the way God receives those whom He saves, giving them not a meagre measure of grace, but manifesting an overflowing love.

This much kissing means, further, much love *perceived*. When his father kissed him much, the poor prodigal knew, if never before, that his father loved him. He had no doubt about it; he had a clear perception of it. It is very frequently the case that the first moment a sinner believes in Jesus, he gets this "much" love. God reveals it to him, and he perceives it and enjoys it at the very beginning. Think not that God always keeps the best wine to the last; He gives us some of the richest dainties of His table the first moment we sit there.

I recollect the joy that I had when first I believed in Jesus; and, even now, in looking back upon it, the memory of it is as fresh as if it were but yesterday. Oh, I could not have believed that a mortal could be so happy after having been so long burdened, and so terribly cast down! I did but look to Jesus on the cross, and the crushing load was immediately gone; and the heart which could only sigh and cry by reason of its burden, began to leap and dance and sing for joy. I had found in Christ all that I wanted, and I rested in the love of God at once. So may it be with you also, if you will but return to God through Christ. It shall be said of you as of this prodigal, "The father saw him, and ran, and fell on his neck, and kissed him in much love."

II. Secondly, this much kissing meant MUCH FORGIVENESS. The prodigal had many sins to confess; but before he came to the details of them, his father had forgiven him. I love confession of sin after forgiveness. Some suppose that after we are forgiven we are never to confess; but, oh, beloved, it is then that we confess most truly, because we know the guilt of sin most really! Then do we plaintively sing—

> "My sins, my sins, my Saviour,
>   How sad on Thee they fall!
> Seen through Thy gentle patience,
>   I tenfold feel them all.
> I know they are forgiven,
>   But still their pain to me
> Is all the grief and anguish
>   They laid, my Lord, on Thee."

To think that Christ should have washed me from my sins in His own blood, makes me feel my sin the more keenly, and confess it the more humbly before God. The picture of this prodigal is marvellously true to the experience of those who return to God. His father kissed him with the kiss of forgiveness; and yet, after that, the young man went on to say, "Father, I have sinned against heaven, and before thee, and am no more worthy to be called thy son." Do not hesitate, then, to acknowledge your sin to God, even though you know that in Christ it is all put away.

From this point of view, those kisses meant first, "*Your sin is all gone*, and will never be mentioned any more. Come to my heart, my son! Thou hast grieved me sore, and angered me; but, as a thick cloud, I have blotted out thy transgressions, and as a cloud thy sins."

As the father looked upon him, and kissed him much, there probably came another kiss, which seemed to say, "*There is no soreness left*: I have not only forgiven, but I have forgotten too. It is all gone, clean gone. I will never accuse you of it any more. I will never love you any the less. I will never treat you as though you were still an unworthy and untrustworthy person." Probably at that there came another kiss; for do not forget that his father forgave him "and kissed him much," to show that the sin was all forgiven.

There stood the prodigal, overwhelmed by his father's goodness, yet remembering his past life. As he looked on himself, and thought, "I have these old rags on still, and I have just come from feeding the swine," I can imagine that his father would give him another kiss, as much as to say, "My boy, I do not recollect the past; I am so glad to see you that *I do not see any filth on you, or any rags on you either.* I am so delighted to have you with me once more that, as I would pick up a diamond out of the mire, and be glad to get the diamond again, so do I pick you up, you are so precious to me." This is the gracious and glorious way in which God treats those who return to Him. As for their sin, He has put it away so that He will not remember it. He forgives like a God. Well may we adore and magnify His matchless mercy as we sing—

> "In wonder lost, with trembling joy
>   We take the pardon of our God;
> Pardon for crimes of deepest dye;
>   A pardon bought with Jesus' blood;
> Who is a pardoning God like Thee
> Or who has grace so rich and free?"

"Well," says one, "can such a wonderful change ever take place with me?" By the grace of God it may be experienced

by every man who is willing to return to God. I pray God
that it may happen now, and that you may get such assurance
of it from the Word of God, by the power of His Holy Spirit,
and from a sight of the precious blood of Christ shed for your
redemption, that you may be able to say, "I understand it
now; I see how He kisses all my sin away; and when it rises,
He kisses it away again."

III. These repeated kisses meant, next, FULL RESTORATION.
The prodigal was going to say to his father, "Make me as one
of thy hired servants." In the far country he had resolved to
make that request, but his father, with a kiss, stopped him.
By that kiss, his *sonship was owned*; by it the father said to the
wretched wanderer, "You are my son." He gave him such
a kiss as he would only give to his own son.

I wonder how many here have ever given such a kiss to anyone.
There sits one who knows something of such kisses as the prodigal
received. That father's girl went astray, and, after years of
sin, she came back worn out, to die at home. He received her,
found her penitent, and gladly welcomed her to his house.
Ah, my dear friend, you know something about such kisses
as those! And you, good woman, whose boy ran away, you
can understand something about these kisses, too. He left you,
and you did not hear of him for years, and he went on in a very
vicious course of life. When you did hear of him, it well-nigh
broke your heart, and when he came back, you hardly knew
him. Do you recollect how you took him in? You felt that
you wished that he was the little boy you used to press to your
bosom; but now he was grown up to be a big man and a great
sinner, yet you gave him such a kiss, and repeated your welcome
so often, that he will never forget it, nor will you forget it either.

You can understand that this overwhelming greeting was like
the father saying, "My boy, you are my son. Despite all that
you have done, you belong to me; however far you have gone
in vice and folly, I own you. You are bone of my bone, and
flesh of my flesh." In this parable Christ would have you know,
poor sinner, that God will own you, if you come to Him confessing your sin through Jesus Christ. He will gladly receive
you; for all things are ready against the day that you return.

> "Spread for thee the festal board,
> See with richest dainties stored,
> To thy Father's bosom pressed,
> Yet again a child confessed;
> Never from His house to roam,
> Come and welcome, sinner, come."

The father received his son with many kisses, and so proved
that his *prayer was answered*. Indeed, his father heard his prayer

before he offered it. He was going to say, "Father, I have sinned," and to ask for forgiveness; but he got the mercy, and a kiss to seal it, before the prayer was presented. This also shall be true of thee, O sinner, who art returning to thy God, through Jesus Christ! You shall be permitted to pray, and God will answer you. Hear it, poor, despairing sinner, whose prayer has seemed to be shut out from heaven! Come to your Father's bosom now, and He will hear your prayers; and, before many days are over, you shall have the clearest proofs that you are fully restored to the divine favour by answers to your intercessions that shall make you marvel at the Lord's loving-kindness to you.

In this repeated kissing we see, then, these three things: much love, much forgiveness, and full restoration.

IV. But these many kisses meant even more than this. They revealed his father's exceeding joy. The father's heart is overflowing with gladness, and he cannot restrain his delight. I think he must have shown his joy by a *repeated look*. His heart beats fast; he feels very joyful; the old man would like the music to strike up; he wants to be at the dancing; but meanwhile he satisfies himself by a repeated look at his long-lost child. Oh, I believe that God looks at the sinner, and looks at him again, and keeps on looking at him, all the while delighting in the very sight of him, when he is truly repentant, and comes back to his Father's house.

The repeated kiss meant, also, a *repeated blessing*, for every time he put his arms round him, and kissed him, he kept saying, "Bless you; oh, bless you, my boy!" He felt that his son had brought a blessing to him by coming back, and he invoked fresh blessings upon his head. Oh, sinner! If you did but know how God would welcome you, and how He would look at you, and how He would bless you, surely you would at once repent, and come to His arms and heart, and find yourself happy in His love.

The many kisses meant, also, *repeated delight*. It is a very wonderful thing that it should be in the power of a sinner to make God glad. He is the happy God, the source and spring of all happiness; what can we add to His blessedness? And yet, speaking after the manner of men, God's highest joy lies in clasping His wilful Ephraims to His breast, when He has heard them bemoaning themselves, and has seen them arising and returning to their home. God grant that He may see that sight even now, and have delight because of sinners returning to Himself! Yea, we believe it shall be even so, because of His presence with us, and because of the gracious working of the Holy Spirit. Surely that is the teaching of the prophet's words:

"The Lord thy God in the midst of thee is mighty; He will save, He will rejoice over thee with joy; He will rest in His love, He will joy over thee with singing." Think of the eternal God singing, and remember that it is because a wandering sinner has returned to Him that He sings. He joys in the return of the prodigal, and all heaven shares in His joy.

V. I have not got through my subject yet. As we take a fifth look, we find that these many kisses mean OVERFLOWING COMFORT. This poor young man, in his hungry, faint, and wretched state, having come a very long way, had not much heart in him. His hunger had taken all energy out of him, and he was so conscious of his guilt that he had hardly the courage to face his father; so his father gives him a kiss, as much as to say, "Come, boy, do not be cast down; I love you."

"Oh, *the past, the past,* my father!" he might moan, as he thought of his wasted years; but he had no sooner said that than he received another kiss, as if his father said, "Never mind the past; I have forgotten all about that." This is the Lord's way with His saved ones. Their past lies hidden under the blood of atonement. The Lord saith by His servant Jeremiah, "The iniquity of Israel shall be sought for, and there shall be none; and the sins of Judah, and they shall not be found: for I will pardon them whom I reserve."

But then, perhaps, the young man looked down on his foul garments, and said, "*The present,* my father, *the present,* what a dreadful state I am in!" And with another kiss would come the answer, "Never mind the present, my boy. I am content to have thee as thou art. I love thee." This, too, is God's word to those who are "accepted in the Beloved." In spite of all their vileness, they are pure and spotless in Christ, and God says of each one of them, "Since thou wast precious in My sight, thou hast been honourable, and I have loved thee. Therefore, though in thyself thou art unworthy, through My dear Son thou art welcome to My home."

"Oh, but," the boy might have said, "*the future,* my father, *the future!* What would you think if I should ever go astray again?" Then would come another holy kiss, and his father would say, "I will see to the future, my boy; I will make home so bright for you that you will never want to go away again." But God does more than that for us when we return to Him. He not only surrounds us with tokens of His love, but He says concerning us, "They shall be My people, and I will be their God: and I will give them one heart, and one way, that they may fear Me for ever, for the good of them, and of their children after them: and I will make an everlasting covenant with them, that I will not turn away from them, to do them good; but

I will put My fear in their hearts, that they shall not depart from me." Furthermore, He says to each returning one, "A new heart also will I give you, and a new spirit will I put within you: and I will take away the stony heart out of your flesh, and I will give you an heart of flesh. And I will put my spirit within you, and cause you to walk in My statutes, and ye shall keep My judgments, and do them."

Whatever there was to trouble the son, the father gave him a kiss to set it all right; and, in like manner, our God has a love-token for every time of doubt and dismay which may come to His reconciled sons. Perhaps one whom I am addressing says, "Even though I confess my sin and seek God's mercy, I shall still be in sore trouble, for through my sin, I have brought myself down to poverty." "There is a kiss for you," says the Lord: "Thy bread shall be given thee, and thy water shall be sure." "But I have even brought disease upon myself by sin," says another. "There is a kiss for you, for I am Jehovah-Rophi, the Lord that healeth thee, who forgiveth all thine iniquities, who healeth all thy diseases." "But I am dreadfully down at the heel," says another. The Lord gives you also a kiss, and says, "I will lift you up, and provide for all your needs. No good thing will I withhold from them that walk uprightly." All the promises in this Book belong to every repentant sinner, who returns to God believing in Jesus Christ, His Son.

VI. And now for our sixth head, though you will think I am getting to be like the old Puritans with these many heads. But I cannot help it, for these many kisses had many meanings: love, forgiveness, restoration, joy, and comfort were in them, and also STRONG ASSURANCE.

The father kissed his son much to make him quite certain that it was *all real*. The prodigal, in receiving these many kisses, might say to himself, "All this love must be true, for a little while ago I heard the hogs grunt, and now I hear nothing but the kisses from my dear father's lips." So his father gave him another kiss, for there was no way of convincing him that the first was real like repeating it; and if there lingered any doubt about the second, the father gave him yet a third. If, when the dream of old was doubted, the interpretation was sure, these repeated kisses left no room for doubt. The father renewed the tokens of his love that his son might be fully assured of its reality.

He did it that in the future it might *never be questioned*. Some of us were brought so low before we were converted, that God gave us an excess of joy when He saved us, that we might never forget it. Sometimes the devil says to me, "You are no child of God." I have long ago given up answering him, for I find that it is a waste of time to argue with such a crafty old liar as he is; he knows too much for me. But if I must answer him, I say, "Why, I remember when I was saved by the Lord! I never can forget even the very spot of ground where first I saw my Saviour; there and then my joy rolled in like some great Atlantic billow, and burst in mighty foam of bliss, covering all things. I cannot forget it." That is an argument which even the devil cannot answer, for he cannot make me believe that such a thing never happened. The Father kissed me much, and I remember it full well. The Lord gives to some of us such a clear deliverance, such a bright, sunshiny day at our conversion, that henceforth we cannot question our state before Him, but must believe that we are eternally saved.

The father put the assurance of this poor returning prodigal beyond all doubt. If the first kisses were given privately, when only the father and son were present, it is quite certain that, afterwards, he kissed him *before men*, where others could see him. He kissed him much in the presence of the household, that they also might not be calling in question that he was his father's child. It was a pity that the elder brother was not there also. You see, he was away in the field. He was more interested in the crops than in the reception of his brother. But the father, when he received that son of his, intended all to know, once for all, that he was indeed his child. Oh, that you might get these many kisses even now! If they are given to you, you will have, for the rest of your life, strong assurance derived from the happiness of your first days.

VII. I have done when I have said that I think that here we have a specimen of the INTIMATE COMMUNION which the Lord often gives to sinners when first they come to Him. "His father saw him, and had compassion, and ran, and fell on his neck, and kissed him much."

You see, this was *before the family fellowship*. Before the servants had prepared the meal, before there had been any music or dancing in the family, his father kissed him. He would have cared little for all their songs, and have valued but slightly his reception by the servants, if, first of all, he had not been welcomed to his father's heart. So is it with us; we need first to have fellowship with God before we think much of union with His people. Before I go to join a church, I want my Father's kiss. Before the pastor gives me the right hand of fellowship, I want my heavenly Father's right hand to welcome me. Before I become recognized by God's people here below, I want a private recognition from the great Father above; and that He gives to all who come to Him as the prodigal came to his father. May He give it to some of you now!

This kissing, also, was *before the table communion.* You know that the prodigal was afterwards to sit at his father's table, and to eat of the fatted calf; but before that, his father kissed him. He would scarcely have been able to sit easily at the feast without the previous kisses of love. The table communion, to which we are invited, is very sweet. To eat the flesh and drink the blood of Christ, in symbol, in the ordinance of the Lord's Supper, is, indeed, a blessed thing; but I want to have communion with God by the way of the love-kiss before I come there. "Let him kiss me with the kisses of his mouth." This is something private, ravishing, and sweet. God give it to many of you! May you get the many kisses of your Father's mouth before you come into the church, or to the communion table!

These many kisses likewise came *before the public rejoicing.* The friends and neighbours were invited to share in the feast. But think how shamefaced the son would have been in their presence, if, first of all, he had not found a place in his father's love, or had not been quite sure of it. He would almost have been inclined to run away again. But the father had kissed him much, and so he could meet the curious gaze of old friends with a smiling face, until any unkind remarks they might have thought of making died away, killed by his evident joy in his father.

It is a hard thing for a man to confess Christ if he has not had an overwhelming sense of communion with Him. But when we are lifted to the skies in the rapture God gives to us, it becomes easy, not only to face the world, but to win the sympathy of even those who might have opposed themselves. This is why young converts are frequently used to lead others into the light; the Lord's many kisses of forgiveness have so recently been given to them, that their words catch the fragrance of divine love as they pass the lips just touched by the Lord. Alas, that any should ever lose their first love, and forget the many kisses they have received from their heavenly Father!

Lastly, all this was given *before the meeting with the elder brother.* If the prodigal son had known what the elder brother thought and said, I should not have wondered at all if he had run off, and never come back at all. He might have come near home, and then, hearing what his brother said, have stolen away again. Yes, but before that could happen, his father had given him the many kisses. Poor sinner! You have come in here, and perhaps you have found the Saviour. It may be that you will go and speak to some Christian man, and he will be afraid to say much to you. I do not wonder that he should doubt you, for you are not, in yourself, as yet a particularly nice sort of person to talk to. But, if you get your Father's many kisses, you will not mind your elder brother being a little hard upon you.

Young Christians are often frightened when they come across some who, from frequent disappointment of their hopes, or from a natural spirit of caution, or perhaps from a lack of spiritual life, receive but coldly those upon whom the Father has lavished much love. If that is your case, never mind these cross-grained elder brethren; get another kiss from your Father. Perhaps the reason it is written, "He kissed him *much*," was because the elder brother, when he came near him, would treat him so coldly, and so angrily refuse to join in the feast.

Lord, give to many poor trembling souls the will to come to Thee! Bring many sinners to Thy blessed feet, and while they are yet a great way off, run and meet them; fall on their neck, give them many kisses of love, and fill them to the full with heavenly delight, for Jesus Christ's sake! Amen.

JESUS AT BETHESDA; OR WAITING CHANGED
FOR BELIEVING

A Sermon

Text.—"After this there was a feast of the Jews; and Jesus went up to Jerusalem. Now there is at Jerusalem by the sheep market a pool, which is called in the Hebrew tongue Bethesda, having five porches. In these lay a great multitude of impotent folk, of blind, halt, withered, waiting for the moving of the water. For an angel went down at a certain season into the pool, and troubled the water: whosoever then first after the troubling of the water stepped in was made whole of whatsoever disease he had. And a certain man was there, which had an infirmity thirty and eight years. When Jesus saw him lie, and knew that he had been now a long time in that case, he saith unto him, Wilt thou be made whole? The impotent man answered him, Sir, I have no man, when the water is troubled, to put me into the pool: but while I am coming, another steppeth down before me. Jesus saith unto him, Rise, take up thy bed, and walk. And immediately the man was made whole, and took up his bed, and walked: and on the same day was the sabbath."—John v. 1–9.

THE scene of this miracle was Bethesda, a pool, according to the evangelist, adjoining the sheep market, or near to the sheep gate: the place through which, I suppose, the cattle consumed by the inhabitants of Jerusalem would be driven; and the pool where, perhaps, the sheep intended for sale to the offerers in the temple were washed. So common was sickness in the days of the Saviour, that the infirmities of men intruded upon the place which had been allotted to cattle, and the place where sheep had been washed, became the spot where sick folk congregated in great multitudes, longing for a cure.

We might never have heard of Bethesda, if an august Visitor had not condescended to honour it with His presence—Jesus, the Son of God, walked in the five porches by the pool. It was the place where we might expect to meet Him, for where should the physician be found if not in the place where the sick are gathered? Here was work for Jesus' healing hand and restoring word. It was but natural that the Son of Man, who "came to seek and to save that which was lost," should make His way to the lazar-house by the side of the pool.

My brethren, Jesus will be here among us also, for there are those who know Him and have power with Him, who have been asking for His presence. The Lord's favoured people, by

prevailing cries and tears, have won from Him His consent to
be in our midst this day, and He is walking amid this throng
as ready to heal and as mighty to save as in the days of His
flesh. "Lo, I am with you always, even unto the end of the
world," is an assurance which comforts the preacher's heart this
morning. A present Saviour—present in the power of the Holy
Ghost—shall make this day to be remembered by many who
shall be made whole.

I ask the earnest attention of all, and I entreat of believers
their fervent assisting prayers while I first bid you observe *the
sick man*; secondly, direct your attentive eye to *the Great
Physician*; and, thirdly, *make an application of the whole narrative
to the present case*.

I. In order to observe THE PATIENT, I shall ask you to go
with me to the pool with the five porches, around which the
sick are lying. Walk tenderly amongst the groups of lame and
blind! Nay, do not close your eyes. It will do you good to
see the sorrowful sight, to mark what sin has done and to what
sorrows our father Adam has made us heirs.

Why are they all here? They are here because sometimes
the waters bubble up with a healing virtue. Whether visibly
stirred by an angel or not it is not necessary for us here to dis-
cuss; but it was generally believed that an angel descended
and touched the water—this rumour attracted the sick from all
quarters. As soon as the stir was seen in the waters, the whole
mass probably leaped into the pool—those who could not leap
themselves were pushed in by their attendants. Alas! how
small the result! Many were disappointed; only one was re-
warded for the leap; whosoever *first* stepped in was healed, but
only the first. For the poor and meagre chance of winning
this cure the sick folk lingered in Bethesda's arches year after
year. The impotent man in the narrative had most likely spent
the better part of his thirty-eight years in waiting at this famous
pool, buoyed up by the slender hope that he might one day
be first of the throng. On the Sabbath mentioned in the text,
the angel had not come to him, but something better had come,
for Jesus Christ, the angel's Master, was there.

Note concerning this man that *he was fully aware of his sickness*.
He did not dispute the failure of his health: he was an impotent
man; he felt it and he owned it. He was not like some present
this morning, who are lost by nature, but who do not know it,
or will not confess it. He was conscious that he needed heavenly
help, and his waiting at the pool showed it. Are there not many
in this assembly who are equally convinced on this point? You
have for a long time felt that you are a sinner, and have known
that unless grace shall save you, saved you never can be. You

are no atheist, no denier of the gospel; on the contrary, you firmly believe the Bible, and heartily wish that you had a saving part in Christ Jesus; but for the present you have advanced no further than to feel that you are sick, to desire to be healed, and to own that the cure must come from above. So far, so good, but it is not good to stop here.

The impotent man thus desiring to be healed, *waited by the pool*, expecting some sign and wonder. He hoped that an angel would suddenly burst open the golden gates and touch the waters which were now calm and stagnant, and that then he might be healed. This, too, my dear hearers, is the thought of many of those who feel their sins and who desire salvation. They accept that unscriptural and dangerous advice given to them by a certain class of ministers; they wait at the pool of Bethesda; they persevere in the formal use of means and ordinances, and continue in unbelief, expecting some great thing. They abide in a continued refusal to obey the gospel, and yet expect that on a sudden they will experience some strange emotions, singular feelings, or remarkable impressions; they hope to see a vision, or hear a supernatural voice, or be alarmed with deliriums of horror.

Now, dear friends, we shall not deny that a few persons have been saved by very singular interpositions of God's hand, in a manner altogether out of the ordinary modes of divine procedure. We should be very foolish if we were for instance to dispute the truth of such a conversion as that of Colonel Gardiner, who, the very night when he made an appointment to commit sin, was arrested and converted by a vision of Christ upon the cross, which, at any rate, he thought he saw, and by hearing or imagining that he heard the voice of the Saviour tenderly pleading with him. It were idle to dispute that such cases have occurred, do occur, and may occur again. I must, however, beg unconverted people not to look for such interpositions in their own cases. When the Lord bids you believe in Jesus, what right have you to demand signs and wonders instead? Jesus Himself is the greatest of all wonders. My dear hearer, for you to wait for remarkable experiences is as futile as was the waiting of the multitude who lingered at Bethesda waiting for the long-expected angel, when He who could heal them stood already in their midst, neglected and despised by them. What a piteous spectacle, to see them gazing into the clouds when the physician who could heal them was present, and they offered Him no petitions, and sought no mercy at His hands.

In dealing with the method of waiting to see or to feel some great thing, we remark, that *it is not the way which God has bidden His servants preach.* I challenge the whole world to find any

gospel of God in which an unconverted man is told to abide
in unbelief. Where is the sinner told to wait upon God in the
use of ordinances, that so he may be saved? The gospel of our
salvation is this—"Believe in the Lord Jesus Christ, and thou
shalt be saved." When our Lord gave His commission to His
disciples, He said, "Go ye into all the world, and preach the
gospel to every creature." And what was that gospel? Tell
them to wait in their unbelief in the use of means and ordinances till they see some great thing? Tell them to be diligent
in prayer, and read the Word of God, until they feel better?
Not an atom of it. Thus saith the Lord, "he that believeth
and is baptized shall be saved; but he that believeth not shall
be damned." This was the gospel, and the only gospel which
Jesus Christ ever bade His ministers preach, and they who say,
wait for feelings! wait for impressions! wait for wonders! they
preach another gospel which is not another; but there be some
that trouble you. The lifting up of Christ on the cross is the
saving work of the gospel ministry, and in the cross of Jesus
lies the hope of men. "Look unto me and be ye saved, all the
ends of the earth," is God's gospel: "Wait at the pool," is man's
gospel, and has destroyed its thousands.

If God had said, "Sit in those seats and wait," I would be
bold to urge it upon you with tears; but God has not said so;
He has said, "Let the wicked forsake his way, and the unrighteous
man his thoughts; and let him return unto the Lord, and he
will have mercy upon him." He has not said "Wait," but He
has said, "Seek ye the Lord while he may be found, call ye
upon him while he is near." "To-day if ye will hear his voice,
harden not your hearts." I find Jesus saying nothing to sinners
about waiting, but very much about coming. "Come unto me,
all ye that labour and are heavy-laden, and I will give you
rest." "If any man thirst, let him come unto me and drink."
"The Spirit and the bride say, Come. And let him that heareth
say, Come. And let him that is athirst come. And whosoever
will, let him take the water of life freely."

Why is this way so very popular? It is because *it administers
laudanum to the conscience.* When the minister preaches with power,
and the hearer's heart is touched, the devil says, "Wait for a
more convenient season." Thus the arch enemy pours this
deadly drug into the soul, and the sinner instead of trusting in
Jesus on the spot, or on bended knee with tearful eye, crying
for mercy, flatters himself because he is in the use of the means:
which use of means is well enough as far as it goes, but which
is bad as bad can be when it comes into the place of Christ
crucified. A child ought to hear its parent's command, but
what if the child puts hearing into the place of obeying? God

forbid that I should glory in your listening to the gospel, if you are hearers only—my glory is in the cross; and unless you look to the cross, it were better for you that you had never been born.

I ask the candid attention of every one who has thus been waiting, while I mention one or two points. My dear friend, is not this waiting *a very hopeless business* after all? Out of those who waited at Bethesda, how very few were ever healed! He who stepped down *first* into the pool was cured, but all the rest came up from the pool just as they went in. Ah! my hearers, I tremble for some of you—you chapel-goers and church-goers, who have for years been waiting, how few of you get saved! Thousands of you die in your sins, waiting in wicked unbelief. A few are snatched like brands from the burning, but the most of those who are hardened waiters, wait, and wait, till they die in their sins. I shall put it to you in God's name, what right have you to expect that if you wait another thirty years, you will be at all different from what you are now? Are not the probabilities most strong that at sixty you will be as graceless as you are at thirty? Is it not time that something better were tried than merely waiting for the troubling of the water? Is it not time that you remembered that Jesus Christ is ready to save you now, and that if you now trust in him, you shall this day have everlasting life?

There lies our poor friend, still waiting at the water's edge. I do not blame *him* for waiting, for Jesus had not been there before, and it was right for him to seize even the most slender chance of a cure; but it was sad that Jesus should have been so slighted: there He went, threading His way through the blind, and the halt, and the lame, and looking benignly upon them all, but none looking up to Him. Now, in other places, soon as Jesus made His appearance, they brought the sick in their beds and laid them at His feet, and as He went along He healed them all, scattering mercies with both His hands. A blindness had come over these people at the pool; there they were, and there was Christ, who could heal them, but not a single one of them sought Him. Their eyes were fixed on the water, expecting it to be troubled; they were so taken up with their own chosen way that the true way was neglected. No mercies were distributed, for none were sought.

Ah! my friends, my sorrowful question is, *shall it be so this morning?* The living Christ is still among us in the energy of His eternal Spirit. Will you be looking to your good works? Will you be trusting to your church-goings and your chapel-goings? Will you rely upon expected emotions, impressions, and fits of terror, and let Christ, who is able to save to the uttermost, have no glimpse of faith, from any eye, no prayer of desire from any heart? If it shall be so, it is heart breaking to think of it; men, with an Almighty Physician in their house, dying while they are amused with a hopeless quackery of their own inventing. O poor souls, shall Bethesda be repeated here this morning, and Jesus Christ, the present Saviour, be again neglected?

If a king should give to one of his subjects a ring, and say to him, "When you are in distress or disgrace, simply send me that ring, and I will do all for you that is needful," if that man should wilfully refuse to send it, but purchase presents, or go about to do some singular feats of valour in order to win his monarch's favour, you would say, "What a fool he is; here is a simple way, but he will not avail himself of it, he wastes his wits in inventing new devices, and toils away his life in following out plans that must end in disappointment." Is not this the case with all those who refuse to trust Christ? The Lord has assured them that if they trust Jesus, they shall be saved; but they go about after ten thousand imaginings, and let their God, their Saviour, go.

Do not, I pray you, play with time any longer. Say not "There is time enough"; for the wise man knows that time enough is little enough. Be not like the foolish drunkard who, staggering home one night, saw his candle lit for him. "Two candles!" said he, for his drunkenness made him see double, "I will blow out one," and as he blew it out, in a moment he was in the dark. Many a man sees double through the drunkenness of sin—he thinks that he has one life to sow his wild oats in, and then the last part of life in which to turn to God; so, like a fool, he blows out the only candle that he has, and in the dark he will have to lie down for ever. Haste thee, traveller, thou hast but one sun, and when that sets, thou wilt never reach thy home. God help thee to make haste now!

II. Let us look at THE PHYSICIAN Himself.

As we have already seen, our Lord on this occasion walked, forgotten and neglected, through that throng of impotent folk, no one crying, "Thou Son of David, have mercy upon me!" no struggling woman seeking to touch the hem of His garment, that she might be made whole! All were desirous of being healed, but, either no one knew or no one trusted Him. What a strange, soul-sickening sight it was, for Jesus was quite able and willing to heal, and to do it all without fee or reward, and yet none sought to Him. Is this scene to be repeated this morning? Jesus Christ is able to save you, my hearers. There is no heart so hard that He cannot soften it; there is no man among you so lost that Jesus cannot save him. Blessed be my dear Master, no case ever did defeat Him; His mighty power reaches beyond the uttermost of all the depths of human sin and folly. If there be a harlot here, Christ can cleanse her. If there be a drunkard or a thief here, the blood of Jesus can make him white as snow. If you have any desire towards Him, you have not gone beyond the reach of His pierced hand. If you are not saved, it is certainly not for want of power in the Saviour.

Moreover, your poverty is no hindrance, for my Master asks nothing from you—the poorer the wretch, the more welcome to Christ. My Master is no covetous priest, who demands pay for what he does—He forgives us freely; He wants none of your merits, nothing whatever from you; come as you are to Him, for He is willing to receive you as you are.

But here is my sorrow and complaint, that this blessed *Lord Jesus, though present to heal, receives no attention from the most of men.* They are looking another way, and have no eyes for Him. *Yet Jesus was not angry.* I do not find that He upbraided one of those who lay in the porches, or that He even thought a hard thought of them; but I am sure that He pitied them, and said in His heart, "Alas! poor souls, that they should not know when mercy is so near!" My Master is not wrathful with you who forget Him and Neglect Him, but He pities you from His heart. I am but His poor servant, but I pity, from my inmost heart, those of you who live without Christ. I could fain weep for you who are trying other ways of salvation, for they will all end in disappointment, and if continued in, will prove to be your eternal destruction.

Observe very carefully what the Saviour did. Looking around amongst the whole company, *He made an election.* He had a right to make what choice He pleased, and He exercised that sovereign prerogative. The Lord is not bound to give His mercy to every one, or to any one. He has freely proclaimed it to you all; but as you reject it, He has now a double right to bless His chosen ones by making them willing in the day of His power. The Saviour selected that man out of the great multitude, we know not why, but certainly for a reason founded in grace. If we might venture to give a reason for His choice it may be that He selected him because his was the worst case, and he had waited the longest of all. This man's case was in everybody's mouth. They said, "This man has been there eight and thirty years."

Our Lord acted according to His own eternal purpose, doing as He pleased with His own; He fixed the eye of His electing love upon that one man, and, going up to him, He gazed upon him. He knew all his history; He knew that he had been a long time in that case, and therefore He pitied him much. He thought of those dreary months and years of painful disappointment which the impotent man had suffered, and the tears were in the Master's eyes; He looked and looked again at that man, and His bowels yearned towards him. Now, I know not whom Christ intends to save this morning by His effectual grace. I am bound to give the general call, it is all that I can do, but I know not where the Lord will give the effectual call, which alone can make the word saving. I should not wonder if He should call some of you who have been waiting long. I will bless His name if He does. I should not marvel if electing love should pitch upon the chief of sinners this day; if Jesus should look on some of you who never looked on Him, until His look shall make *you* look, and His pity shall make you have pity upon yourselves, and His irresistible grace shall make you come to Him that you may be saved.

Jesus, having looked upon this man with a special eye of regard, said to him, "Wilt thou be made whole?" This was not said because Christ wanted information, but because He wished to *arouse the man's attention*. On account of its being the Sabbath, the man was not thinking of being cured, for to the Jew it seemed a most unlikely thing that cures should be wrought on a Sabbath day. Jesus, therefore, brought his thoughts back to the matter in hand; for, mark you, the work of grace is a work upon a conscious mind, not upon senseless matter. Though Puseyites pretend to regenerate unconscious children, by sprinkling their faces with water, Jesus never attempted such a thing —Jesus saves men who have the use of their senses—and His salvation is a work upon a quickened intellect and awakened affections. Jesus brought back the wandering mind with the question, "Wilt thou be made whole?" "Indeed," the man might have said, "indeed, I desire it above all things—I long for it—I pant for it."

Now, my dear hearer, I will ask the same question of you. "Wilt thou be made whole? Do you desire to be saved? Do you know what being saved is?" "Oh," say you, "it is escaping from hell." No, no, no; that is the result of being saved, but being saved is a different thing. Do you want to be saved from the power of sin? Do you desire to be saved from being covetous, worldly-minded, bad-tempered, unjust, ungodly, domineering, drunken, or profane? Are you willing to give up the sin that is dearest to you? "No," says one, "I cannot honestly say I desire all that." Then, you are not the man I am seeking this morning: but is there one here who says, "Yes, I long to be rid of sin, root and branch; I desire, by God's grace, this very day to become a Christian, and to be saved from sin"?

Well, then, as you are already in a state of thoughtfulness, let us go a step further, and observe what the Saviour did. *He*

gave the word of command, saying, "Rise! take up thy bed and walk."
The power by which the man arose was not in himself, but in
Jesus; it was not the mere sound of the word which made him
rise, but it was the divine power which went with it. I do believe
that Jesus still speaks through His ministers; I trust that He
speaks through *me* at this moment, when in His name I say to
you who have been waiting at the pool, wait no longer, but
this moment believe in Jesus Christ! Trust Him now. I know
that my word will not make you do it; but if the Holy Ghost
works through the word, you will believe. Trust Christ now,
poor sinner. Believe that He is able to save you; believe it now!
Rely upon Him to save you this moment; repose upon Him
now! If you are enabled to believe, the power will come from
Him, not from you; and your salvation will be effected, not by
the sound of the word, but by the secret power of the Holy
Ghost which goes with that word.

I pray you observe, that although nothing is said about faith
in the text, yet *the man must have had faith.* Suppose you had been
unable to move hand or foot for thirty-eight years, and some
one said at your bedside, "Rise!" you would not think of trying to rise, you would know it to be impossible; you must have
faith in the person who uttered the word, or else you would
not make the attempt. I think I see the poor man—there he is,
a heap, a writhing bundle of tortured nerves and powerless
muscles; yet Jesus says, "Rise!" and up he rises in a moment.
"Take up thy bed," says the Master, and the bed is carried.
Here was the man's faith. The man was a Jew, and he knew
that, according to the Pharisees, it would be a very wicked
thing for him to roll up his mattress and carry it on the Sabbath;
but because Jesus told him, he asked no questions, but doubled
up his couch, and walked. He did what he was told to do,
because he believed in Him who spake. Have *you* such faith in
Jesus, poor sinner? Do you believe that Christ can save you?
If you do, then I say to you in His name, trust Him! Trust
Him now! If you trust Jesus, you shall be saved this morning
—saved on the spot, and saved for ever.

Observe, beloved friends, that *the cure which Christ wrought was
perfect.* The man could carry his bed; the restoration was proved
to a demonstration, the cure was manifest; all could see it.
Moreover, the cure was *immediate.* He was not told to take a
lump of figs, and put it on the sore, and wait; he was not carried home by his friends, and laid up for a month or two, and
gradually nursed into vital energy. Oh, no! he was cured there
and then. Half our professing Christians imagine that regeneration cannot take place in a moment; and, therefore, they say
to poor sinners, "Go and lie at Bethesda's pool; wait in the

use of ordinances; humble yourself; seek for deeper repentance."
Beloved, away with such teaching! The cross! the cross! the
cross! there hangs a sinner's hope! You must not rely on what
you can do, nor on what angels can do, nor on visions and
dreams, nor on feelings and strange emotions, and horrible
deliriums, but you must rest in the blood of my Master and
my God, once slain for sinners. There is life in a look at the
Crucified One, but there is life nowhere else. I come to the
same point, then, upon the second head as the first. Thus saith
the Lord, "Look unto me, and be ye saved, all the ends of the
earth."

III. Thirdly, we have to APPLY THE INSTANCE IN THE TEXT
TO THE PRESENT OCCASION.

Let me talk with you who doubt this matter. You still think
that you must wait—you have had a sufficient spell of waiting,
and you are getting tolerably weary, but still you stick to the
old plan; hopeless as it is, you still catch at it as drowning men
do at straws. But I want to show you that this is all wrong.
Regeneration is an instantaneous work, and justification an
instantaneous gift. *Man fell in a moment.* When Eve plucked
the fruit, and Adam ate it, it did not require six months to
bring them into a state of condemnation. It did not require
several years of continued sin to cast them out of paradise.
Their eyes were opened by the forbidden fruit; they saw that
they were naked, and they hid themselves from God. Surely,
surely, Christ is not to be longer about His work than the devil
was about his. Shall the devil destroy us in a moment, and
Jesus be unable to save us in a moment! Ah! glory be to God,
He has power to deliver far more ample than any which Satan
uses for man's destruction.

Look at the *Biblical illustrations* of what salvation is. I will
only mention three. Noah built an ark; that was the type of
salvation; now, when was Noah saved? Christ has built the
ark for us, we have nothing to do with building that; but when
was Noah saved? Does any one say, "He was safe after he had
been in the ark a month and had arranged all the things and
looked out on the deluge and felt his danger?" No! the moment
Noah went through the door, and the Lord shut him in, Noah
was safe. When he had been in the ark a second he was as secure
as when he had been there a month.

Take the case of the passover, when were the Jews safe from
the destroying angel who went through the land of Egypt?
Were they safe after the blood which was sprinkled on the door
had been looked upon and considered for a week or two? Oh,
no! beloved, the moment the blood was sprinkled the house was
secured; and the moment a sinner believes and trusts in the

crucified Son of God he is pardoned at once, he receives salvation in full through Christ's blood.

One more instance, the brazen serpent. When the brazen serpent was lifted up, what were the wounded to do? Were they told to wait till the brazen serpent was pushed into their faces, or until the venom of the serpent showed certain symptoms in their flesh? No, they were commanded to look. They did look. Were they healed in six months' time? I read not so, but as soon as their eye met the serpent of brass, the cure was wrought; and as soon as your eye meets Christ, poor trembler, you are saved. Though yesterday you were deep in your cups, and up to your neck in sin, yet if this morning you look to my once slain but now exalted Master, you shall find eternal life.

Again take *Biblical instances*. Did the dying thief wait at the pool of the ordinances? You know how soon his believing prayer was heard, and Jesus said, "To-day shalt thou be with me in paradise." The three thousand at Pentecost, did they wait for some great thing? Nay, they believed, and were baptized. Look at the jailer of Philippi. It was the dead of the night, the prison was shaken, and the jailer was alarmed, and said, "Sir, what must I do to be saved?" Did Paul say, "Well, you must use the means and look for a blessing upon the ordinances"? No! he said, "Believe in the Lord Jesus Christ, and thou shalt be saved, and thy house," and that very night he baptized him. Paul did not take the time about it that some think so exceedingly necessary. He believed as I do, that there is life in a look at Jesus; he bade men look, and looking they lived.

Possibly you will see this still more clearly if I remind you that *the work of salvation is all done*. There is nothing for a sinner to do in order to be saved, it is all done for him. You want washing. The bath does not need filling. "There is a fountain filled with blood." You want clothing. You have not to make the garment, the robe is ready. The garment of Christ's righteousness is woven from the top throughout, all that is wanted is to have it put on. If some work remained for you to do it might be a lengthened process, but all the doing is accomplished by Christ. Salvation is not of works, but of grace, and to accept what Christ presents you is not a work of time.

Once more, let me say to you that *regeneration itself cannot be a work of a long time*, because, even where it seemed to be most gradual, when looked at closely, it turns out in its essence to be the work of a moment. There is a dead man: now, if that man be raised from the dead, there must be an instant in which he was dead, and another instant in which he was alive. The actual quickening must be the work of a moment. I grant you that at the first the life may be very feeble, but there must be a

time when it begins. There must be a line—we cannot always
see it ourselves, but God must see it—there must be a line between life and death. A man cannot be somewhere between
dead and alive; he either is alive or he is dead; and so you are
either dead in sin or alive unto God, and quickening cannot
involve a long period of time.

Finally, my hearers, *for God to say, "I forgive thee," takes not a
century nor a year*. The judge pronounces the sentence, and the
criminal is acquitted. If God shall say to thee this morning,
"I absolve thee," thou art absolved, and thou mayest go in
peace. I must bear faithful witness as to my own case. I never
found mercy by waiting. I never obtained a gleam of hope by
depending upon ordinances. I found salvation by believing. I
heard a simple minister of the gospel say, "Look and live!
Look to Jesus! He bleeds in the garden, He dies on the tree!
Trust Him! Trust to what He suffered instead of you; and if
you trust Him, you shall be saved." The Lord knows I had
heard that gospel many times before, but I had not obeyed it.
It came, however, with power to my soul, and I did look, and
the moment I looked to Christ, I lost my burden.

"But," says one, "how do you know?" Did you ever carry
a burden yourself? "Oh, yes," say you. Did you know when
it was off? "How did you know?" "Oh," you say, "I felt so
different. I knew when my burden was on, and, consequently,
I knew when it was off." It was so in my case. I only wish
some of you felt the burden of sin as I felt it, when I was waiting
at the pool of Bethesda. I wonder that such waiting had not
landed me in hell. But, when I heard the word, "Look!" I
looked, and my burden was gone. I wondered where it was
gone; I have never seen it since, and I never shall see it again.
It went into the Master's tomb, and it lies for ever buried there.
God has said it, "I have blotted out like a cloud thine iniquities,
and like a thick cloud thy sins."

Oh, come, ye needy, come to my Master! Ho, ye that have
been disappointed with rites and ceremonies, and feelings, and
impressions, and all the hopes of the flesh, come at my Master's
command, and look up to Him! He is not here in the flesh,
for He has risen; but He has risen to plead for sinners, and
"he is able to save them to the uttermost that come unto God
by him, seeing he ever liveth to make intercession for them."

Let me say, solemnly, to you who have heard the word this
day, I have told you the plan of salvation plainly; if you do
not accept it, I am clear of your blood, I shake my skirts of the
blood of your souls. The Lord save each one of you, and His
shall be the praise ever more. Amen.

A SERMON TO OPEN NEGLECTERS AND NOMINAL FOLLOWERS OF RELIGION

A Sermon

Text.—"But what think ye? A certain man had two sons; and he came to the first, and said, Son, go work to day in my vineyard. He answered and said, I will not: but afterward he repented, and went. And he came to the second and said likewise. And he answered and said, I go, sir: and went not. Whether of them twain did the will of his father? They say unto him, The first. Jesus saith unto them, Verily I say unto you, That the publicans and the harlots go into the kingdom of God before you. For John came unto you in the way of righteousness, and ye believed him not: but the publicans and the harlots believed him: and ye, when he had seen it, repented not afterwards, that ye might believe him."—Matthew xxi. 28–32.

In this crowded assembly, I hope there are hundreds, if not thousands, who would be prepared to die for our Lord Jesus; and in yonder crowded seats, we may count by hundreds those who bear the name and accept the gospel of the Man of Nazareth; and yet, I fear me, that there are many enemies of the Son of God, who are forgetful of His righteous claims—who have cast from them those cords of love which should bind them to His throne, and have never submitted to the mighty love which showed itself in His cross and in His wounds. I cannot attempt the separation. You must grow together until the harvest. To divide you were a task which at this hour angels could not perform, but which one day they will easily accomplish, when at their Master's bidding, the harvest being come, they shall gather together first the tares in bundles to burn them, and afterwards the wheat into Jehovah's barn. I shall not attempt the division, but I shall ask each man to attempt it for himself in his own case.

Let each man question himself this morning, "Am I on the Lord's side? Am I for Christ, or for his enemies? Do I gather with him, or do I scatter abroad?" "Divide! divide!" they say in the House of Commons; let us say the same in this great congregation this day. Political divisions are but trifles compared with the all-important distinction which I would have you consider. Divide as you will be divided to the right and to the left in the great day when Christ shall judge the world in righteousness. Divide as you will be divided when the bliss of heaven, or the woes of hell, shall be your everlasting portion.

I trust I was guided by the Spirit of God to my text this morning, for it is of such a character, that while it enables me to address the whole mass of the unconverted, it gives me a hopeful opportunity of getting at the conscience of each by dividing the great company of the unconverted into two distinct classes. O that for each tribe of unbelievers, there may be a blessing in store this day.

First, we shall speak to *those who are avowedly disobedient to God;* and, secondly, to those who are *deceptively submissive to Him.*

I. First, we have a word for THOSE WHO ARE AVOWEDLY DISOBEDIENT TO GOD. There are many such here. God has said to you as He says to all who hear the gospel, "Son, go work to-day in my vineyard"; and you have replied, perhaps honestly, but certainly very boldly, very unkindly, very unjustly, "I will not." You have made no bones about it, but given a refusal point-blank to the claims of your Creator. You have spoken your mind right out, not only in words, but in a more forcible and unmistakable manner, for actions speak far more loudly than words. You have said, over and over again, by your actions, "I will not serve God, or believe in His Son Jesus."

My dear friend, I am glad to see you here this morning, and trust that matters will change with you ere you leave; but at present you have not yielded even an outward obedience to God, but in all ways have said, "I will not."

Moreover, my friend, you have not as yet given an assent to the doctrines of God's Word; on the contrary, *intellectually* as well as practically, you go not at God's bidding. You have set up in your mind the idea that you must understand everything before you will believe it—an idea, let me tell you, which you will never be able to carry out, for you cannot understand your own existence; and there are ten thousand other things around you which you never can comprehend, but which you must believe or remain for ever a gigantic fool. Still you cavil at this doctrine and that doctrine, railing at the gospel system in general. Let me say on my own account, that as far as I am personally concerned, it is a very small consideration to me whether you do like my doctrine or do not; for your own sake I am anxious above measure that you should believe the truth as it is in Jesus; but while you live in sin, your dislike of a doctrine, will very probably only make me feel the more sure of its truth, and lead me to preach it with more confidence and vehemence.

Ah souls! we have some higher end to be served than merely pleasing you. We would save you by distasteful truths, for honeyed lies will ruin you. That teaching which the carnal mind most delights in, is the most deadly and delusive. With many of you, your beliefs, and tastes, and likes, must be changed, or else you will never enter heaven. I admit that in a measure I like your honesty in having said outright, "I will not serve God"; but it is an honesty which makes me shudder, for it betrays a heart hard as the nether millstone.

Again, you have said, "I will not serve God," and up to this time it is very possible that you have never been in the humour to repent of having said it, for the ways of sin are sweet to you, and your heart is fixed in its rebellion. You have never felt that conviction of sin which the Holy Spirit has wrought in some of us; if you had felt it, you would soon have been shaken out of your "I will not." If God's power of grace, of which thousands of us bear witness that it is as real a power as that which guides the stars or wings the wind—if God's almighty grace should once get a hold of you, you would no longer say, "I do not believe this or that"; for, as tremblingly as any of those whom you now despise, you would cry out, "What must I do to be saved?"

The answer of the son to his father as recorded in our text was very plain; it was not, however, very genuine, or such as his father might have expected. His father said, "Son, go work to-day in my vineyard"; and the son rudely said, "I will not, that is flat"; and without another word of apology or reason went his way. This is not quite as it should be. Is it? Even so, my friend, you may have been too hasty and so have been unjust. Is it not very possible you have denied to God and to His gospel the respect which both really deserve? You have spoken very plainly, but at the same time very thoughtlessly, very harshly to the God who has deserved better things of you. Have you ever given the claims of the Lord Jesus a fair consideration? Have you not dismissed the gospel with a sneer quite unworthy of you? Have you not been afraid to look the matters between God and your soul fairly in the face? I believe it to be the case of hundreds here; I know it to be the case of thousands and tens of thousands in London. They have put their foot down, and they have said, "None of your religion for me! I have made up my mind and I will never alter; I hate it and will not listen to it." Does no small voice within ever tell them that this is not fair to themselves or to God? Is the matter so easily to be decided? Suppose it should turn out that the religion of Jesus is true, what then? What will be the lot of those who despised Him? My hearer, the religion of Jesus is true, and I have proved its truth in my own case; do, I pray you, consider it, and do not trifle away your immortal soul. Thus saith the Lord, "Consider your ways."

It is now time for me to tell the openly ungodly what is his real estate. You have been more than a little proud of your honesty; and looking down upon certain professers of religion you have said, "Ah! I make no such pretences as they do, I am honest, I am." Friend, you cannot have a greater abhorrence of hypocrites than I have; if you can find a fair chance of laughing at them, pray do so. If by any means you can stick pins into their wind-bags, and let the gas of their profession out, pray do so. I try to do a little of it in my way, do you do the same!

You and I are agreed in this, I hope, in heartily hating anything like sham and falsehood; but if you begin to hold your head up, and think yourself so very superior because you make no profession, I must take you down a little by reminding you that it is no credit to a thief that he makes no profession of being honest, and it is not thought to be exceedingly honourable to a man that he makes no profession of speaking the truth. For the fact is, that a man who does not profess to be honest is a professed thief, and he who does not claim to speak the truth is an acknowledged liar; thus in escaping one horn you are thrown upon another, you miss the rock but run upon the quick sand. You are a confessed and avowed neglecter of God, a professed despiser of the great salvation, an acknowledged disbeliever in the Christ of God.

Yet I came not here to tell you of your sins only, but to help you to escape from them. It is necessary that this much should be said, but we now turn to something far more pleasant. I am in hopes this day that some of you will listen to that little word in the text, "*Afterward.*" He said, "I will not; but *afterward* he repented, and went." It is a long lane which has no turning, let us trust that we have come to the turning now. There is space left you for repentance; though you may have been a drunkard, or a swearer, or unchaste, the die is not yet cast, a change is yet possible. May God grant that you may have reached the time when it shall be said of you, "Afterward he repented; he changed his mind; he believed upon Jesus, and obeyed the word of the Lord, and went."

Perhaps the son in the parable thought a little more calmly about it. He said to himself, "I will consider the matter, second thoughts are often best. I growled at my good father, and gave him a sharp answer, and I saw the tear standing in the good man's eye. I am sorry I grieved him. The thought of grieving him makes me change my mind. I said 'No' to him," said he, "but I did not think about it. I forgot that if I go and work in my father's vineyard, I shall be working for myself, for I am his eldest son, and all that he has will belong to me, so that I am very foolish to refuse to work to my own advantage.

Ah! now I see my father had my advantage at heart, I will even go as he bade me." See, he shoulders his tools, and away he marches to labour with all his might. He said, "I will not," but he repented and went, and it is admitted by all that he did the will of his father.

Oh, I hope that many a man and woman here will this day cry, "I do retract what I have said. I will go to my Father, and will say to Him, 'I will do Thy bidding. I will not grieve Thy love. I will not lose the opportunity of advancing my soul's best interest; I obey the gospel command.'" I will suppose that I see one such before me, and I will speak to him. Perhaps he said, "I will not," because he really did not understand what religion was. How few after all know what the way of salvation is; though they go to church, and to chapel, they have not yet learned God's plan of pardoning sinners.

Do you know the plan of salvation? Hear it and live by it. You have offended God; God must punish sin; it is a fixed law that sin must be punished; how then can God have mercy upon you? Why, only in this way: Jesus Christ came from heaven and He suffered in the room, place, and stead of all who trust Him; suffered what they ought to have suffered, so that God is just, and yet at the same time He is able to forgive the very chief of sinners through the merits of His dear Son. Your debts, if you be a believer in Him, Christ has paid on your behalf. If you do but come and rest upon Jesus and upon Jesus only, God cannot punish you for your sins, for He punished Jesus for them, and it would not be just of Him to punish Christ and then to punish you, to exact payment first from the Surety and afterwards from the debtor.

My dear hearer, whoever thou mayst be, whatever thy past life may have been, if thou wilt trust Christ, thou shalt be saved from all thy sin in a moment, the whole of thy past life shall be blotted out; there shall not remain in God's book so much as a single charge against thy soul, for Christ who died for thee, shall take thy guilt away and leave thee without a blot before the face of God. Read the last verse of my text, and you will see that it was by believing that men entered into the kingdom of God of old, and it is still by believing that men are saved. "Behold the Lamb of God," said John the Baptist, and if you look to that bleeding Lamb, you shall live. Do you understand this? Is it not simple? Is it not suitable to you? Will you still refuse to obey it? Does not the Holy Spirit prompt you to relent? Do you not even now say, "Is it so simple? I will even trust in Jesus:

> 'Guilty, but with heart relenting,
> To the Saviour's wounds I'll fly.'

I will come, by God's help, this morning, lest death should come before the sun sets. I will trust Christ to save me. Precious way of salvation! Why should I not be saved?"

It is possible too, that you may have said, "I will not," because you really thought there was no hope for you. Ah! my friend, let me assure you—and oh! how glad I am to be able to do it—that there is hope for the vilest through the precious blood of Jesus. No man can have gone too far for the long arm of Christ to reach him. Christ delights to save the biggest sinners. He said to His apostles, "Preach the gospel to every creature, but begin"—where? "begin at Jerusalem. There live the wretches who spat in My face. There live the cruel ones that drove the nails through My hands. Go and preach the gospel to them first. Tell them that I am able to save, not little sinners merely, but the very chief of sinners. Tell them to trust in Me and they shall live." Where are you, you despairing one? I know the devil will try to keep the sound of the gospel from your ears if he can, and therefore, I would "cry aloud and spare not." O ye despairing sinners, there is no room for despair this side the gates of hell. If you have gone through the foulest kennels of iniquity, no stain can stand out against the power of the cleansing blood.

> "There is a fountain filled with blood,
>   Drawn from Immanuel's veins,
> And sinners plunged beneath that flood,
>   Lose ALL their guilty stains."

Oh, I trust, now that you know there is hope for you, you will say, "I will even come at once, and put my trust in Jesus."

While I would thus encourage you to repent of your neglect of God, let me invite you to come to Jesus, and press it upon you yet again. Ah! my dear friend, you will soon be dying, and though some wicked men, in their stupid insensibility, die very calmly, and as David said, "They are not in trouble as other men, neither are they plagued like other men, but their strength is firm," yet, whether they perceive it or not, it is a dreadful thing to die with unpardoned sin hanging about you. What will your guilty soul do when it leaves the body? Think of it a minute. It is a matter worthy of your thought. Some of you, in all probability, will die this week. It is not probable that so many thousands of us will march through a whole week, and be found alive at the other end of it. Well, then, as we *may* some of us go soon, and all of us *must* go ere long, let us look before us and think a bit. Imagine your soul unclothed of the body. You have left the body behind you, and your disembodied spirit finds itself in a new world. Oh, it will be a glorious thing if that separated spirit shall see Jesus whom it has loved, and fly at once into His bosom, and drink for ever of the crystal fountain of ever-flowing bliss: but it will be a horrible thing if instead of it, your naked shivering spirit should wake up to find itself friendless, homeless, helpless, hopeless, tormented with remorse, afflicted with despair. What if it should have to cry out for ever, "I knew my duty but I did it not, I knew the way of salvation but I would not run in it. I heard the gospel, but I shut my ears to it. I lived and at length left the world without Christ, and here I am, past hope, no repenting now, no believing now, no escaping now, for mercy and love no longer rule the hour."

Have pity on thyself, my hearer. I have pity on thee. Oh, if my hand could pluck thee from that flame, how cheerfully would I do it! Shall I pity thee and wilt thou not pity thyself? Oh, if my pleadings should by God's grace persuade you to trust in Christ this morning, I would plead with you while voice, and lungs, and heart, and life held out! But oh, have pity on thyself! Pity that poor naked spirit which so soon will be quivering with utmost agony, a self-caused agony, an agony from which it would not escape, an agony of which it was warned, but which it chose to endure sooner than give up sin and yield to the sceptre of sovereign grace.

I would fain hope that you are saying, "I do now repent, and by God's grace I will go." If so, let me tell you there are a great many in heaven who once, like you, said, "I will not," but they afterwards repented and are now saved. I will give you one picture. Yonder, I see a company of men on horseback, and there is one, the proudest of them all, to whom they act as a guard; they are going to Damascus, that he may take Christians to prison and compel them to blaspheme. Saul of Tarsus is the name of that cruel, murderous persecutor. When Stephen was put to death, God said to this man Saul, "Go, work in my vineyard," but Saul said plainly, "I will not," and to prove his enmity, he helped to put Stephen to death. There he is riding in hot haste, upon his evil errand, none more set and determined against the Lord.

Yet my Lord Jesus can tame the lion, and even make a lamb of him. As he rides along, a bright light is seen, brighter than the sun at noonday; he falls from his horse, he lies trembling on the ground, and he hears a voice out of heaven, saying, "Saul, Saul, why persecutest thou me?" Lifting up his eyes with astonishment, he sees that he had ignorantly been persecuting the Son of God. What a change that one discovery wrought in him. That voice, "I am Jesus, whom thou persecutest," broke his hard heart, and won him to the cause. You know how three days after that, that once proud and bigoted man was baptized upon profession of the faith of Christ, whom he had just now persecuted! and if you want to see an earnest preacher, where can you find a better than the apostle Paul, who, with heart on fire, writes again and again, "God forbid that I should glory, save in the cross of our Lord Jesus Christ."

I hope there is a Saul here, who is to be struck down this morning. Lord, strike him down! Eternal Spirit strike him down *now*! You did not know perhaps, that you had been fighting God, but you thought the religion of Jesus to be a foolish dream. You did not know that you had insulted the dying Saviour; now you do know it, may your conscience be affected, and from this day forth may you serve the Lord.

I must leave this second point when I have just said this. If there be one here who after a long refusal, at last relents, and is willing to become a servant of God by faith in Jesus Christ, let me tell him for his encouragement, he shall not be one whit behind those who have been so long making a profession without being true to it, for the text says, "The publicans and harlots go into the kingdom"; but what else? "Go into the kingdom" *before* those who made a profession of serving God, but who were not true to it. You great sinners shall have no back seats in heaven! There shall be no outer court for you. You great sinners shall have as much love as the best, as much joy as the brightest of saints. You shall be near to Christ; you shall sit with Him upon His throne; you shall wear the crown; your fingers shall touch the golden harps; you shall rejoice with the joy which is unspeakable and full of glory. Will ye not come? Christ forgets your past ill manners, and bids ye come to-day. "Come," saith He, "unto me all ye that labour and are heavy laden and I will give you rest." Thirty years of sin shall be forgiven, and it shall not take thirty minutes to do it in. Fifty, sixty, seventy years of iniquity shall all disappear as the morning's hoar-frost disappears before the sun. Come and trust my Master, hiding in His bleeding wounds.

> "Raise thy downcast eyes, and see
>   What throngs His throne surround!
> These, though sinners once like thee,
>   Have full salvation found.
> Yield not then to unbelief;
>   He says, 'There yet is room':
> Though of sinners thou art chief,
>   Since Jesus calls thee, come."

II. Bear with me a little time while I speak to the second character, THE DECEPTIVELY SUBMISSIVE, by far the most numerous everywhere in England, probably the most numerous in this assembly. Oh! you, my own regular hearers, many of you are in this class. You have said to the Great Father, "I go, sir!" but you have not gone. Let me sorrowfully sketch your portraits: you have regularly frequented a place of worship, and you would shudder to waste a single Sunday in an excursion, or in any form of Sabbath breaking. Outwardly you have said, "I go, sir." When the hymn is given out, you stand up and sing, and yet you do not sing with the heart. When I say, "Let us pray!" you cover your faces, but you do not pray with real prayer. You utter a polite, respectful, "I go, sir," but you do not go. You give a notional assent to the gospel. If I were to mention any doctrine, you would say, "Yes, that is true. I believe that." But your heart does not believe: you do not believe the gospel in the core of your nature, for if you did, it would have an effect upon you.

A man may say, "I believe my house is on fire," but if he goes to bed and falls asleep, it does not look as if he believed it, for when a man's house is on fire he tries to escape. If some of you really believed that there is a hell, and that there is a heaven, as you believe other things, you would act very differently from what you now do. I must add that many of you say, "I go, sir," in a very solemn sense, for when we preach earnestly the tears run down your cheeks, and you go home to your bedrooms, and you pray a little, and everybody thinks that your concern of mind will end in conversion: but your goodness is "like the morning clouds and the early dew." You are like dunghills with snow upon them: while the snow lasts you look white and fair, but when the snow melts the dunghill remains a dunghill still.

Oh, how many very impressible hearts are like that! You sin, and yet you come to a place of worship, and tremble under the word; you transgress, and you weep and transgress again; you feel the power of the gospel after a fashion, and yet you revolt against it more and more. Ah! my friends, I can look some of you in the face and know that I am describing some of your cases to the letter. You have been telling lies to God all these years, by saying, "I go, sir," while you have not gone. You know that to be saved you must believe in Jesus, but you have not believed. You know that you must be born again, but you are still strangers to the new birth. You are as religious as the seats you sit on, but no more; and you are as likely to get to heaven as those seats are, but not one whit more, for you are dead in sin, and death cannot enter heaven.

O my dear hearers, I lament that ever I should be called to say such a thing as this, and not be more affected by the fact;

and, wonder of wonders, that you, some of you, know it to be true, and yet do not feel alarmed thereby! It is the easiest thing in the world to impress some of you by a sermon, but, I fear me, you never will get beyond mere transient impressions. Like the water when lashed, the wound soon heals. You know, and you know, and you know; and you feel, and feel, and feel again, and yet your sins, your self-righteousness, your carelessness, or your wilful wickedness, cause you, after having said, "I go, sir," to forget the promise and lie unto God.

Now, I spoke very honestly to the other class, and must be equally plain with you. You, too, *criminate yourselves*. There will be no need of witnesses against you. You have admitted that the gospel is true. You did not quarrel with the doctrine of future punishment or future glory. You attended a place of worship, and you said that God was good and worthy to be served; you confessed that you owed allegiance to Him, and ought to render it. You have even knelt down and in prayer you have said, "Lord, I deserve Thy wrath." The great God has only to turn to some of your formal prayers to find quite enough evidence to secure your condemnation. Those morning prayers of yours, those evening prayers, hypocritical every one of them, will be more than sufficient to condemn you of your own mouth. Take heed! take heed, I pray you, while you are yet in the land of hope.

All this while, as the thirty-second verse reminds me, while you have remained unsaved, you have seen publicans and harlots saved by the very gospel which has had no power upon you. Do not you know it, young man? You, I mean, the son of a godly mother? You know that there have been picked off of the streets poor fallen women who have been brought to know Christ, who are among the sweetest and fairest flowers in Christ's garden now, though they were once castaways; and yet some of you respectable people who never committed any outward vice in your lives, are still unconverted, and still saying to Christ, "I go, sir," but you have not gone. You are still without God! Without Christ! Lost, lost, lost!

Yet fairer outward characters could scarcely be found. I could fain weep for you! Oh! beware, beware of being like the apples of Sodom, which are green to look upon, but when crushed, crumble to ashes. Beware of being like John Bunyan's trees that were green outside, but inwardly rotten, and only fit to be tinder for the devil's tinder-box. Oh! beware of saying as some of you do, "I go, sir," while you go not. I sometimes see sick people who quite alarm and distress me. I say to them, "My dear friend, you are dying; have you a hope?" There is no answer. "Do you know your lost state?" "Yes, sir."

"Christ died for sinners." "Yes, sir." "Faith gives us of His grace." "Yes, sir." They say, "Yes, sir; yes, sir; yes, sir; yes, sir." I sometimes wish before God they would contradict me, for if they would but have honesty enough to say, "I do not believe a word of it," I should know how to deal with them. Stubborn oaks are levelled by the gale, but those who bend like the willow before every wind, what wind shall break them? O dear brethren, beware of being gospel-hardened; or, what is the same thing, softened but for a season. Beware of being a promising hearer of the word, and nothing more!

I do not mean to close my discourse by speaking to you in this apparently harsh way, which, harsh as it seems, is full of love to your soul. I have a good word for *you* too. I trust that you will have a change wrought in you by the Holy Ghost, for although these many years you have made false professions before God, there is yet room in His gospel feast for you. Did you notice the text? "The publicans and sinners enter into the kingdom of heaven *before you*." Then it is clear you may come after them, because it could not be said they entered *before* you, if you did not come after them. If the Lord shall break your heart, you will be willing to take the Lord Jesus for your all in all in just the same way as a drunkard must, though you have not been a drunkard. You will be willing to rest in the merit of Jesus just as a harlot must, though you have never been such. There is room for you, young people, yet, though you have broken your vows, and quenched your convictions. Ay, and you grey-headed people may be brought yet, though you have lived so long in the outward means, but have never given up your hearts to Jesus. Oh, come! May the Lord bring you. In this very place may the Lord lead you to say silently, "By the grace of God I will not be an open pretender any longer; I will give myself up to those dear hands that bled for me, and that dear heart that was pierced for me, and I will this day submit to Jesus' way."

The fact is, to close the subject, there is, my dear friends, the same gospel to be preached to one class of men as to every other class. I pray God the day may never come when we shall be found in our preaching talking about working classes, and middle classes, and upper classes. No, there is but one way of salvation, but one foundation, but one propitiation, but one gospel. Look to the cross of Christ and live. High was the brazen serpent lifted, and all that Moses said was, "Look." Was a prince of the house of Judah bitten, he was told to look; without looking his lion standard of costly emblazonry could not avail him; was some poor wretch in the camp bitten, he must look, and the efficacy was the same for him as for the

greatest of the host. Look! look! look to Jesus. Believe in the
Son of God and live! One brazen serpent for all the camp,
one Christ for all ranks and conditions of men.

What a blessing would it be if we were all enabled to trust
Christ this morning! My brethren, why not? He is worthy of
the confidence of all. The Spirit of God is able to work faith
in all. O poor sinner, look to Him! Dear hearers, I may never
speak to some of you again, and I would therefore be pressing
with you; by the hour of death, by the solemnities of eternity,
I do implore and beseech you accept the only remedy for sin
which even God Himself will ever offer to the dying sons of
men, the remedy of a bleeding Substitute, suffering in your
room and stead, believed on and accepted in the heart. Cast
yourself flat upon Christ. The way of salvation is just this—
rest alone upon Christ! Depend wholly upon Him.

The negro was asked what he did, and he said, "I jest fall
down on de rock, and he dat is down on de rock cannot fall
no lower." Down on the rock, sinner! Down on the rock!
The everlasting rock of ages! You cannot fall lower than that.

I will conclude with a well-known illustration. Your condition
is like that of a child in a burning house, who, having escaped
to the edge of the window, hung on by the window-sill. The
flames were pouring out of the window underneath, and the
poor lad would soon be burnt, or falling would be dashed to
pieces; he therefore held on with the clutch of death. He did
not dare to relax his grasp till a strong man stood underneath,
and said, "Boy! drop! drop! I'll catch you." Now, it was
no saving faith for the boy to believe that the man was strong
—that was a good help towards faith—but he might have known
that and yet have perished; it was faith when the boy let go
and dropped down into his big friend's arms.

There are you, sinner, clinging to your sins or to your good
works. The Saviour cries, "Drop! drop into My arms!" It
is not doing, it is leaving off doing. It is not working, it is trusting
in that work which Jesus has already done. Trust! that is the
word, simple, solid, hearty, earnest trust. Trust and it will
not take an hour to save you, the moment you trust you are
saved. You may have come in here as black as hell, but if you
trust in Jesus you are wholly forgiven. In an instant, swifter
than a flash of lightning the deed of grace is done. O may God
the Spirit do it now, bringing you to trust, that you may be
saved.

JESUS CHRIST HIMSELF

A Sermon

Text.—"Jesus Christ himself."—Ephesians ii. 20.

"Jesus Christ himself" is to occupy all our thoughts this morning. What an ocean opens up before me! Here is sea-room for the largest barque! In which direction shall I turn your thoughts? I am embarrassed with riches. I know not where to begin: and when I once begin where shall I end? Assuredly we need not go abroad for joys this morning, for we have a feast at home. The words are few, but the meaning vast— "Jesus Christ himself."

Beloved, the religion of our Lord Jesus Christ contains in it nothing so wonderful as Himself. It is a mass of *marvels*, but He is THE miracle of it; the wonder of wonders is "The Wonderful" Himself. If *proof* be asked of the truth which He proclaimed, we point men to Jesus Christ Himself. His character is unique. We defy unbelievers to imagine another like Him. He is God and yet man, and we challenge them to compose a narrative in which the two apparently incongruous characters shall be so harmoniously blended,—in which the human and divine shall be so marvellously apparent, without the one overshadowing the other.

They question the authenticity of the four Gospels; will they try and write a fifth? Will they even attempt to add a few incidents to the life which shall be worthy of the sacred biography, and congruous with those facts which are already described? If it be all a forgery, will they be so good as to show us how it is done? Will they find a novelist who will write another biography of a man of any century they choose, of any nationality, or of any degree of experience, or any rank or station, and let us see if they can describe in that imaginary life a devotion, a self-sacrifice, a truthfulness, a completeness of character at all comparable to that of Jesus Christ Himself? Can they invent another perfect character even if the divine element be left out? They must of necessity fail, for there is none like unto Jesus Himself.

The character of Jesus has commanded respect even from those who have abhorred His teaching. It has been a stumblingstone to all objectors who have preserved a shade of candour. Jesus' doctrine they could refute, they say; His precepts they could improve, so they boast; His system is narrow and outworn, so they assert: but Himself—what can they do with Him? They must admire Him even if they will not adore Him; and having done so they have admired a Personage who must be divine, or else He wilfully left His disciples to believe a lie. How will they surmount this difficulty? They cannot do so by railing at Him, for they have no material for accusation. Jesus Christ Himself silences their cavillings. This is a file at which these asps do bite, but break their teeth. Beyond all argument or miracle, Jesus Christ Himself is the proof of His own gospel.

And as He is the proof of it, so, beloved, He is the *marrow* and essence of it. When the apostle Paul meant that the gospel was preached he said, "Christ is preached," for the gospel is Christ Himself. If you want to know what Jesus taught, know Himself. He is the incarnation of that truth which by Him and in Him is revealed to the sons of men. Did He not Himself say, "I am the way, the truth, and the life"? You have not to take down innumerable tomes, nor to pore over mysterious sentences of double meaning in order to know what our great Teacher has revealed, you have but to turn and gaze upon His countenance, behold His actions, and note His spirit, and you know His teaching. He lived what He taught. If we wish to know Him, we may hear His gentle voice saying "Come and see." Study His wounds, and you understand His innermost philosophy. "To know him and the power of his resurrection" is the highest degree of spiritual learning. He is the end of the law and the soul of the gospel, and when we have preached His word to the full, we may close by saying, "Now, of the things which we have spoken this is the sum,—we have an high priest who is set on the right hand of the throne of the majesty in the heavens."

Nor is He alone the proof of His gospel and the substance of it, but He is the *power* and force by which it spreads. When a heart is truly broken for sin, it is by Him that it is bound up. If a man is converted, it is by Christ, the power of God. If we enter into peace and salvation it is by the gracious manifestation of Jesus Himself. If men have enthusiastically loved Christianity, it is because first of all they loved Christ: for Him apostles laboured, and for Him confessors were brave; for Him saints have suffered the loss of all things, and for Him martyrs have died. The power which creates heroic consecration is "Jesus Christ himself." The memories stirred by His name have more influence over men's hearts than all things else in earth or heaven. He causes the wheel of providence to revolve in such a manner as to help His cause; He abridges the power of tyrants, overrules the scourge of war, establishes liberty in nations, opens the mysteries of continents long unknown, breaks down systems of error, and guides the current of human thought. He works by a thousand means, preparing the way of the Lord.

It is from heaven that He shall shortly come, and when He cometh, when Christ Himself shall put forth all His might, then shall the wilderness rejoice and the solitary place be glad. The reserve force of the gospel is Christ Jesus Himself. The latent power which shall at last break every bond, and win universal dominion, is the energy, the life, the omnipotence of Jesus Himself. He sleeps in the vessel now, but when He arises and chides the storm there will be a deep calm. He now for awhile concealeth Himself in the ivory palaces of glory, but when He is manifested in *that day* His chariot wheels shall bring victory to His church militant.

If these things be so, I have a theme before me which I cannot compass. I forbear the impossible task, and I shall but briefly note some few apparent matters which lie upon the surface of the subject.

Brethren, "Jesus Christ himself" should always be the prominent thought of our minds as Christians. Our theology should be framed upon the fact that He is the Centre and Head of all. We must remember that "in him are hid all the treasures of wisdom and knowledge." Jesus Christ Himself is to us precept, for He is the way: He is to us doctrine, for He is the truth: He is to us experience, for He is the life. Let us make Him the pole star of our religious life in all things. Let Him be first, last, and midst; yea, let us say, "He is all my salvation and all my desire." And yet do not, I beseech you, disdain the doctrine, lest in marring the doctrine you should be guilty of insult to Jesus Himself.

To trifle with truth is to despise Jesus as our Prophet. Do not for a moment underrate experience, lest in neglecting the inner self you also despise your Lord Himself as your cleansing Priest; and never for a moment forget His commandments lest if ye break them ye transgress against Jesus Himself as your King. All things which touch upon His Kingdom are to be treated reverently by us for the sake of Himself: His book, His day, His Church, His ordinances, must all be precious to us, because they have to do with Him; but in the front of all must ever stand "Jesus Christ himself," the personal, living, loving Jesus; Christ in us the hope of glory, Christ for us our full redemption, Christ with us our guide and our solace, and Christ above us pleading and preparing our place in heaven. Jesus Christ Himself is our captain, our armour, our strength, and our victory. We inscribe His name upon our banner, for it is hell's terror, heaven's delight, and earth's hope. We bear this upon our hearts in the heat of the conflict, for this is our breastplate and coat of mail.

I. With Jesus Christ Himself we begin by saying, first, that Jesus Himself is THE ESSENCE OF HIS OWN WORK, and therefore *how readily we ought to trust Him.* Jesus Himself is the soul of His own salvation. How does the apostle describe it? "He loved me, and gave *himself* for me." He gave His crown, His throne, and His joys in heaven for us, but that was not all—he gave Himself. He gave His life on earth, and renounced all the comforts of existence, and bore all its woes; He gave His body, He gave His agony, He gave His heart's blood: but the summary of it is, He gave Himself for me. "Christ loved the church and gave himself for it." "Who his own self bare our sins in his own body on the tree." No proxy service here! No sacrifice which runs as far as His own person and there stops! There was no limit to the grief of Jesus like that set upon the suffering of Job,—"Only on himself lay not thine hand," or "Only spare his life." No, every reserve was taken down, for He gave Himself. "He saved others; himself he could not save," because He Himself was the very essence of His own sacrifice on our behalf. It is because He is what He is that He was able to redeem us: the dignity of His person imparted efficacy to His atonement. He is divine, God over all, blessed for ever, and therefore infinite virtue is found in Him; He is human, and perfect in that humanity, and therefore capable of obedience and suffering in man's place and stead. He is able to save us because He is Immanuel—"God with us." If it were conceivable that an angel could have suffered the same agonies, and have performed the same labours, as our Lord, yet it is not conceivable that the same result would have followed.

The pre-eminence of His person imparted weight to His work. Always think then when you view the atonement, that it is Jesus Himself who is the soul of it. Indeed the efficacy of His sacrifice lies there; hence the apostle in the Hebrews speaks of Him as having "by himself purged our sins." This purging was wrought by His sacrifice, but the sacrifice was Himself. Paul says, "he offered up himself." He stood as a priest at the altar offering a bloody sacrifice, but the offering was neither bullock, nor ram, nor turtle dove; it was Himself. "Once in the end of the world hath he appeared to put away sin by the sacrifice of himself." The sole reason why we are well-pleasing with God is because of Him, for He is our sweet savour-offering; and the only cause for the putting away of our sin is found in Him because He is our sin-offering. The cleansing by the blood, and the washing by the water, are the result, not of the blood and the water in and of themselves and separate from Him, but because they were the essentials of Himself.

Now, because of this, *the Lord Jesus Christ Himself is the object of our faith.* Is He not always so described in Scripture? "Look unto *me*, and be ye saved, all ye ends of the earth,"—not "look to my cross," nor "look to my life," nor "to my death," much less "to my sacraments or to my servants," but "look unto *me*." From His own lips the words sound forth, "Come *unto me* all ye that labour and are heavy laden, and I will give you rest." In fact, it is the Christian's life motto, "Looking unto Jesus, the author and finisher of our faith."

May I not go further and say, *how very simple and how very easy and natural ought faith to be henceforth?* I might be puzzled with various theories of the atonement, but I can believe in Jesus Himself: I might be staggered by the divers mysteries which concern theology, and overpower even master-minds, but I can confide in Jesus Himself. He is one whom it is difficult to distrust: His goodness, gentleness, and truth command our confidence. We can and do trust in Jesus Himself. If He be proposed to me as my Saviour, and if faith in Him be that which saves me, then at His dear feet I cast myself unreservedly, and feel myself secure while He looks down on me. He Who bled that sinners might be saved cannot be doubted any more: "Lord, I believe; help thou mine unbelief."

Now you who have been looking to your faith, I want you to look to Jesus Himself rather than at your poor feeble faith. Now you who have been studying the results of faith in yourselves and are dissatisfied, I beseech you turn your eyes away from yourselves and look to Jesus Himself. Now you who cannot understand this and cannot understand that, give up wanting to understand for the while, and come and look at Jesus Christ Himself, "that the God of our Lord Jesus Christ, the Father of glory, may give unto you the spirit of wisdom and revelation in the knowledge of him." The Lord grant us grace to view Jesus Christ Himself in the matter of our salvation as all in all, so that we may have personal dealings with Him, and no more think of Him as a mere idea, or as an historical Personage, but as a personal Saviour standing in the midst of us, and bidding us enter into peace through Him.

II. "Jesus Christ himself" is as we have said THE SUBSTANCE OF THE GOSPEL, *and therefore how closely should we study Him.* While He was here He taught His disciples, and *the object of His teaching was that they might know Himself,* and through Him might know the Father. They did not learn very fast, but you see what He meant them to learn by the observation He made to Philip, "Have I been so long time with you, and yet hast thou

not known *me*, Philip?" He meant them to know Himself;
and when He had risen from the dead the same object was
still before Him. As He walked with the two disciples to Em-
maus they had wide choice of subjects for conversation, but
He chose the old theme, and "beginning at Moses and all the
prophets, he expounded unto them in all the Scriptures the
things concerning himself." Our Lord was concerned to be
known to His people, and therefore again and again we read
that "Jesus showed himself unto his disciples." Whatever else
they may be ignorant of, it is essential to disciples that they
know their Lord. His nature, His character, His mind, His
spirit, His object, His power, we must know—in a word, we
must know Jesus Himself.

This also, beloved, is the work of the Holy Spirit. "He shall glorify
me: for he shall receive of mine, and shall shew it unto you."
The Holy Ghost reveals Christ to us and in us. Whatsoever
things Christ hath spoken while He was here, the Holy Ghost
opens to the mind and to the understanding, and thus by speaking of Christ within us He carries on the work which our Lord
began when here below. The Comforter is the instructor and
Jesus is the lesson. I dare say you long to know a thousand
things, but the main point of knowledge to be desired is Jesus
Himself.

This was His teaching, and this is the Holy Spirit's teaching,
and *this is the end and object of the Bible.* Moses, Esaias, and all
the prophets spake of Him, and the things which are recorded
in this book were written that ye might believe that Jesus is
the Christ, and that believing ye might have life through His
name. Precious is this book, but its main preciousness lies in
its revealing Jesus Himself, it is the field which contains the
pearl of great price, the casket which encloses heaven's brightest
jewel. We have missed our way in the Bible if its silken clue
has not led us to the central chamber where we see Jesus Himself. We have never been truly taught of the Holy Ghost, and
we have missed the teaching of the life of Christ, unless we
have come to abide in Jesus Himself. To know Him is our
beginning of wisdom and our crown of wisdom. To know Him
is our first lesson on the stool of penitence and our last attainment as we enter heaven. Our ambition is that we may know
the love of Christ which passeth knowledge. Here is our life
study, and we have good associates in it, for these things the
angels desire to look into. May the Lord grant that the eyes
of your understanding may be enlightened, that we may know
what is the hope of His calling and what the riches of the glory
of His inheritance in the saints.

Beloved, because Jesus is the sum of the gospel *He must be our constant theme.* "God forbid that I should glory save in the cross of our Lord Jesus Christ." "I determined not to know anything among you save Jesus Christ and him crucified." So spake men of old, and so say we. When we have done preaching Christ we had better have done preaching; when you have done teaching in your classes Jesus Christ Himself, give up Sunday school work, for nothing else is worthy of your pains. Put out the sun, and light is gone, life is gone, all is gone. When Jesus is pushed into the background or left out of a minister's teaching, the darkness is darkness that might be felt, and the people escape from it into gospel light as soon as they can.

A sermon without Jesus in it is savourless, and worthless to God's tried saints, and they soon seek other food. The more of Christ in our testimony the more of light and life and power to save. Some preachers are guilty of the most wearisome tautology, but this is not laid to their charge when their theme is Jesus. I have heard hearers declare that their minister appeared to have bought a barrel organ on which he could grind five or six tunes and no more, and these he ground out for ever and ever, amen. They have been weary, very weary, of such vain repetitions; but to this day I never heard of anybody against whom the complaint was urged that he preached Christ too much, too often, too earnestly, or too joyfully. I never recollect seeing a single Christian man coming out of a congregation with a sorrowful face saying, "He extolled the Redeemer too highly: he grossly exaggerated the praises of our Saviour."

I do not remember ever meeting with a case in which the sick upon the bed of languishing have complained that thoughts of Jesus were burdensome to them. I never recollect that a single book has been denounced by earnest Christian men because it spoke too highly of the Lord, and made Him too prominent. No, my brethren, He Who is the study of the saints must be the daily theme of ministers if they would feed the flock of God. No theme so moves the heart, so arouses the conscience, so satisfies the desires, and so calms the fears. God forbid we should ever fail to preach Jesus Himself. There is no fear of exhausting the subject, nor of our driving away our hearers, for His words are still true, "I, if I be lifted up, will draw all men unto me."

III. Jesus Christ himself is THE OBJECT OF OUR LOVE, and *how dear He should be,* We can all of us who are really saved declare that "We love him because he first loved us." We have an intense affection for His blessed person as well as gratitude for His salvation. The personality of Christ is a fact always to be kept prominently in our thoughts. The love of a truth is all very well, but the love of a person has far more power in it. We have heard of men dying for an idea, but it is infinitely more easy to awaken enthusiasm for a person. When an idea becomes embodied in a man it has a force which in its abstract form it never wielded. Jesus Christ is loved by us as the embodiment of everything that is lovely, and true, and pure, and of good report. He Himself is incarnate perfection, inspired by love. We love His offices, we love the types which describe Him, we love the ordinances by which He is set forth, but we love Himself best of all. He Himself is our beloved; our heart rests only in Him.

Because we love Him we love His people, and through Him we enter into union with them. Our text is taken from a verse which says, "Jesus Christ himself being the chief corner stone." He is the binder at the corner, joining Jew and Gentile in one temple. In Jesus those ancient differences cease, for he "hath made both one, and hath broken down the middle wall of partition between us; to make in himself of twain one new man, so making peace." We are at one with every man who is at one with Christ. Only let our Lord say, "I love that man," and we love him at once; let us only hope that our friend can say, "I love Jesus," and we hasten to respond, "And I love you for Jesus' sake." So warm is the fire of our love to Jesus that all His friends may sit at it, and welcome. Our circle of affection comprehends all who in any shape or way have truly to do with Jesus Himself.

Because we love Himself we delight to render service to Him. Whatever service we do for His church, and for His truth, we do for His sake, even if we can only render it to the least of His brethren we do it unto Him. The woman with the alabaster box of precious ointment is a type which we greatly prize, for she would only break the precious box *for Him,* and every drop of its delicious contents must be poured only upon His head. The bystanders complained of waste, but there can be no waste in anything that is done for Jesus. If the whole world, and the heavens, and the heaven of heavens were all one great alabaster box, and if all the sweets which can be conceived were hived within it, we would wish to see the whole broken, that every drop of the sweetness might be poured out for Jesus Christ Himself.

> "Jesus is worthy to receive
> Honour and power divine;
> And blessings more than we can give,
> Be Lord, for ever Thine."

Oh our Beloved, if we can do anything for Thee, we are charmed at possessing such a privilege. If we are allowed to wash Thy disciples' feet, or to care for the poorest of Thy poor, or the least lamb of Thy flock, we accept the office as a high honour, for we love Thee with all our hearts. Our love to Jesus should be as much a matter of fact as our affection for our husband, wife, or child, and it should be far more influential upon our lives. Love to our Lord is, I trust, moving all of you to personal service. You might have paid a subscription and allowed others to work, but you cannot do it when you see that Jesus gave Himself for you. Jesus Himself demands that I myself should be consecrated to His praise. Personal service is due to a personal Christ, who personally loved and personally died for us. When nothing moves us to zeal, when the jaded spirit cannot follow up its industries, let but Jesus Himself appear, and straightway our passions are all in a blaze, and the fiery spirit compels the flesh to warm to its work again. We even glory in infirmity when Jesus is near, and venture upon works which else had seemed impossible. We can do anything and everything for "Jesus Christ himself."

IV. Fourthly, our Lord Jesus Christ Himself is THE SOURCE OF ALL OUR JOY. *How ought we to rejoice when we have such a springing well of blessedness.* In times of sorrow our solace is Jesus Himself. It is no small ground of comfort to a mourner that Jesus Himself is a man. How cheering to read, "Forasmuch as the children are partakers of flesh and blood, he also himself took part of the same." The humanity of Christ has a charm about it which the quietly sorrowful alone discover. I have known what it is to gaze upon the incarnation with calm repose of heart when my brain has seemed to be on fire with anguish. If Jesus be indeed my brother Man, there is hope at all times. This is better balm than that of Gilead, "Himself took our infirmities, and bare our sicknesses"; "For in that he himself hath suffered, being tempted, he is able also to succour them that are tempted." Pain, hunger, thirst, desertion, scorn, and agony Jesus Himself has borne. Tempted in all points like as we are, though without sin, He has become the chief Comforter of the sorrowful. Many and many a sufferer in the lone watches of the night has thought of Him and felt his strength renewed. Our patience revives when we see the Man of Sorrows silent before His accusers. Who can refuse to drink of His cup and to be baptized with His baptism?

> "His way was much rougher and darker than mine:
> Did Christ, my Lord, suffer, and shall I repine?"

The darkness of Gethsemane has been light to many an agonized soul, and the passion even unto death has made the dying sing for joy of heart. Jesus Himself is the solace of our soul in sorrow, and when we emerge from the storm of distress into the deep calm of peace, as we often do, blessed be His name, He is our peace. Peace He left us by legacy, and peace He creates in person. We never know deep peace of heart until we know the Lord Jesus Himself. You remember that sweet word when the disciples were met together, the doors being shut for fear of the Jews, "Jesus himself stood in the midst of them, and said, Peace be unto you." Jesus Himself you see brought the message; for nothing but His presence could make it effectual. When we see Him our spirit smells a sweet savour of rest. Where can an aching head find such another pillow as His bosom?

On high days and holidays our spirits soar beyond rest: we ascend into the heaven of joy and exultation; but then it is our Lord's joy which is in us making our joy full. "Then were the disciples glad when they saw the Lord," and then are we glad also. By faith we see Jesus Himself enthroned, and this has filled us with delight, for His glorification is our satisfaction. "Him also hath God highly exalted, and given him a name which is above every name." I care not what becomes of me so long as He is glorified. The soldier dies happy when the shout of victory salutes his ear, and his failing sight beholds his prince triumphant. What a joy to think that Jesus is risen—risen to die no more: the joy of resurrection is superlative. What bliss to know that He has ascended, leading captivity captive, that He sitteth now enthroned in happy state, and that He will come in all the glory of the Father to break His enemies in pieces as with a rod of iron. Here lies the grandest joy of His expectant church. She has in reserve a mighty thunder of hosannahs for that auspicious day.

V. Fifthly, JESUS CHRIST HIMSELF IS THE MODEL OF OUR LIFE, and therefore *how blessed it is to be like Him.* As to our rule for life, we are like the disciples on the mount of transfiguration when Moses and Elias had vanished, for we see "no man save Jesus only." Every virtue found in other men we find in Him in greater perfection; we admire the grace of God in them, but Jesus Himself is our pattern. It was once said of Henry VIII., by a severe critic, that if the characteristics of all the tyrants that had ever lived had been forgotten, they might all have been seen to the life in that one king: we may more truly say of Jesus, if all graces, and virtues, and sweetnesses which have ever been seen in good men could all be forgotten, you might find them all in Him: for in Him dwells all that is good and great. We, therefore, desire to copy His character and put our feet into His footprints. Be it ours to follow the Lamb whithersoever He goeth. What saith our Lord Himself? "Follow me," and again,

"Take my yoke upon you and learn of me, for I am meek and lowly in heart, and ye shall find rest unto your souls." By the indwelling of the Holy Spirit and His gracious operations we are developing into the image of Christ till Christ be formed in us; and we thus develop because the heavenly life in us is His own life. It is not passing through baptism, nor bearing the name of Christ, it is having Jesus Himself in our hearts that makes us Christians, and in proportion as He is formed in us and the new life grows we become more and more like Him. And this is our prospect for eternity, that we are to be with Him and like Him, for "when he shall appear, we shall be like him, for we shall see him as he is."

Think of Him, you that mourn your imperfectness to-day—think of Jesus Christ Himself, and then be assured that you are to be like Him. What a picture! Come, artist, bring your best skill here. What can you do? All pencils fail to depict *Him*. It needs a poet's eye as well as an artist's hand to picture the Lovely One. But what can the poet do? Ah, you also fail; you cannot sing Him any more than your friend can paint Him. Fruitful conception and soaring imagination may come to your aid, but they cannot prevent your failure. He is too beautiful to be described—He must be seen. Yet here comes the marvel—"We shall be like him"—like Jesus Christ Himself. O saint, when thou art risen from the dead how lovely thou wilt be! Wilt thou know thyself? To-day thou art wrinkled with old age, scarred with the marks of disease and pain, and perhaps deformed by accident, or blanched with consumption, but none of these shall blemish thee then. Thou wilt be without spot or wrinkle, faultless before the throne.

> "O glorious hour! O blest abode!
> I shall be near and like my God."

And not in bodily form alone shall we be like unto Him whose eyes are as the eyes of doves, and whose cheeks are as beds of spices; but in spirit and in soul shall we be perfectly conformed to the Well-beloved. We shall be holy even as He is holy, and happy as He is happy. Christ Himself then becomes to us unspeakably precious, as the model of our present life and the image of the perfection towards which the Holy Ghost is working us.

VI. Lastly, HE IS THE LORD OF OUR SOUL. *How sweet it will be to be with Him.* We find to-day that His beloved company makes everything move pleasantly whether we run in the way of His commands, or traverse the valley of the shadow of death. Saints have lain in dungeons, and yet they have walked at liberty when He has been there; they have been stretched on the rack, and even called it a bed of roses when He has stood by. One lay on a grid-iron, with the hot fires beneath him; but amidst the flames he challenged his tormentors to do their worst, and laughed them to scorn, for his Lord was there. Martyrs have been seen to clap their hands when every finger burned like a lighted candle, and they have been heard to cry, "Christ is all," "Christ is all." When the Fourth, like unto the Son of God, walks in the furnace, all the fire can do is but to snap their bonds and set the sufferers free.

Oh, brethren, I am sure your only happiness that has been worth the having has been found in knowing that He loved you and was near you. We are never right till we come out of ourselves and into Jesus; but when the ecstatic state comes, and we stand right out of self, and stand in Him, so that whether in the body or out of the body we can scarcely tell, God knoweth; then are we getting back to where God meant man to have been when he walked with Him in Eden, getting near to where God means we shall be when we shall see Him face to face. Brethren, what must the unveiled vision be! If the sight of Him here be so sweet, what must it be to see Him hereafter! It may be we shall not live till He cometh, for the Master may tarry; but if He doth not come, and we therefore are called to pass through the gate of death, we need not fear. I should not wonder if when we pass under the veil and come out in the disembodied state, one of our astonishments will be to find Jesus Himself there waiting to receive us. What a glance of love will that be which He will give to us and which we shall return to Him. Shall we ever take our eyes away from Him? Shall we ever wish to do so? Will not the poet's words be true,

"Millions of years my wondering eyes,
    Shall o'er thy beauties rove;
And endless ages I'll adore
    The glories of Thy love."

Within a week it may be our meeting with Jesus Himself may take place; perhaps within an hour. A poor girl lying in the hospital was told by the doctor or the nurse that she could only live another hour; she waited patiently, and when there remained only one quarter of an hour more, she exclaimed: "One more quarter of an hour, and then——" she could not say what, neither can I; only Jesus Himself hath said, "Father, I will that they also, whom thou hast given me, be with me where I am; that they may behold my glory." And as He has prayed, so shall it be, and so let it be. Amen and Amen.

THE DREAM OF PILATE'S WIFE

A Sermon

Text.—"When he was set down on the judgment seat, his wife sent unto him, saying, Have thou nothing to do with that just man: for I have suffered many things this day in a dream because of him."—Matthew xxvii. 19.

I EARNESTLY wished to pursue the story of our Saviour's trials previous to His crucifixion, but when I sat down to study the subject I found myself altogether incapable of the exercise. "When I thought to know this, it was too painful for me." My emotions grew so strong, and my sense of our Lord's grief became so extremely vivid, that I felt I must waive the subject for a time. I could not watch with Him another hour, and yet I could not leave the hallowed scene. It was, therefore, a relief to meet with the episode of Pilate's wife and her dream: it enables me to continue the thread of my narrative, and yet to relax the extreme tension of the feelings caused by a near view of the Master's grief and shame.

My spirit failed before the terrible sight. I thought I saw Him brought back from Herod where the men of war had set Him at nought. I followed Him through the streets again as the cruel priests pushed through the crowd and hastened Him back to Pilate's hall. I thought I heard them in the streets electing Barabbas, the robber, to be set free, instead of Jesus, the Saviour, and I detected the first rising of that awful cry, "Crucify, crucify," which they shrieked out from their blood-thirsty throats: and there He stood, who loved me and gave Himself for me, like a lamb in the midst of wolves, with none to pity and none to help Him.

The vision overwhelmed me, especially when I knew that the next stage would be that Pilate, who had exculpated Him by declaring, "I find no fault in him," would give Him over to the tormentors that He might be scourged, that the mercenary soldiery would crown Him with thorns and mercilessly insult Him, and that He would be brought forth to the people and announced to them with that heart-rending word, "Behold the man!" Was there ever sorrow like unto His sorrow? Rather than speak about it this day, I feel inclined to act like Job's friends, of whom it is written, that at the sight of him "they lifted up their voice, and wept; and sat down with him upon the ground seven days and seven nights, and none spake a word unto him: for they saw that his grief was very great."

We leave the Master a while to look at this dream of Pilate's wife, which is only spoken of once in the Scriptures, and then by Matthew. I know not why that evangelist only should have been commissioned to record it; perhaps he alone heard of it; but the one record is sufficient for our faith, and long enough to furnish food for meditation. We receive the story as certified by the Holy Spirit.

Pilate throughout his term of office had grossly misbehaved himself. He had been an unjust and unscrupulous ruler of the Jews. The Galileans and the Samaritans both felt the terror of his arms; for he did not hesitate to massacre them at the slightest sign of revolt; and among the Jews themselves he had sent men with daggers into the midst of the crowds at the great gatherings, and so had cut off those who were obnoxious to him. Gain was his object, and pride ruled his spirit. At the time when Jesus of Nazareth was brought before him a complaint against him was on the way to Tiberius the Emperor, and he feared lest he should be called to account for his oppressions, extortions, and murders. His sins at this moment were beginning to punish him: as Job would word it, "The iniquities of his heels compassed him about."

One terrible portion of the penalty of sin is its power to force a man to commit yet further iniquity. Pilate's transgressions were now howling around him like a pack of wolves; he could not face them, and he had not grace to flee to the one great refuge; but his fears drove him to flee before them, and there was no way apparently open for him but that which led him into yet deeper abominations. He knew that Jesus was without a single fault, and yet since the Jews clamoured for His death he felt that he must yield to their demands, or else they would raise another accusation against himself, namely, that he was not loyal to the sovereignty of Cæsar, for he had allowed One to escape who had called Himself a king. If he had behaved justly he would not have been afraid of the chief priests and scribes. Innocence is brave; but guilt is cowardly. Pilate's old sins found him out and made him weak in the presence of the ignoble crew, whom otherwise he would have driven from the judgment seat.

The manner and the words of Jesus had impressed Pilate. I say the manner of Jesus, for His matchless meekness must have struck the governor as being a very unusual thing in a prisoner. He had seen in captured Jews the fierce courage of fanaticism; but there was no fanaticism in Christ. He had also seen in many prisoners the meanness which will do or say anything to escape from death; but he saw nothing of that about our Lord. He saw in Him unusual gentleness and humility combined with majestic dignity. He beheld submission blended with innocence. This made Pilate feel how awful goodness is. He was impressed—he could not help being impressed—with this unique sufferer. He felt that he himself was placed in a very extraordinary position, being asked to condemn one whom he knew to be perfectly innocent. His duty was clear enough, he could never have had a question about· that; but duty was nothing to Pilate in comparison with his own interests. He would spare the Just One if he could do so without endangering himself; but his cowardly fears lashed him on to the shedding of innocent blood.

At the very moment when he was vacillating, when he had proffered to the Jews the choice of Barabbas, or Jesus of Nazareth; —at that very moment, I say, when he had taken his seat upon the bench, and was waiting for their choice, there came from the hand of God a warning to him, a warning which would for ever make it clear that, if he condemned Jesus, it would be done voluntarily by his own guilty hands. Jesus must die by the determinate counsel and foreknowledge of God, and yet it must be by wicked hands that He is crucified and slain; and hence Pilate must not sin in ignorance. A warning to Pilate came from his own wife concerning her morning's dream, a vision of mystery and terror, warning him not to touch that just Person; "for," said she, "I have suffered many things this day in a dream because of him."

I. And, first, I call your attention to THE CO-OPERATION OF PROVIDENCE WITH THE WORK OF GOD. I call it the work of God to warn men against sin, and I call your attention to Providence working with it to bring the preventives and cautions of divine mercy home to men's minds.

For, first, observe the providence of God *in sending this dream.* If anything beneath the moon may be thought to be exempt from law, and to be the creature of pure chance, surely it is a dream. True, there were in old time dreams in which God spake to men prophetically; but ordinarily they are the carnival of thought, a maze of mental states, a dance of disorder. The dreams which would naturally come to the wife of a Roman governor would not be likely to have much of tenderness or conscience in them, and would not, in all probability, of themselves run in the line of mercy. Dreams ordinarily are the most disorderly of phenomena, and yet it seems that they are ordered of the Lord. I can well understand that every drop of spray which flashes from the wave when it dashes against the cliff has its appointed orbit as truly as the stars of heaven; but the thoughts of men appear to be utterly lawless, especially the thoughts of men when deep sleep falleth upon them. As well might one foretell the flight of a bird as the course of a dream. Such wild fantasies seem to be ungoverned and ungovernable. Many things operate naturally to fashion a dream. Dreams often owe their shape to the state of the body or the agitation of the mind. Dreams may, no doubt, be caused by that which transpires in the chamber of the house; a little movement of the bed caused by passing wheels, or the tramp of a band of men, or the passing of a domestic across the floor, or even the running of a mouse behind the wainscot, may suggest and shape a dream. Any slight matter affecting the senses at such time may raise within the slumbering mind a mob of strange ideas. Yet whatever may have operated in this lady's case, the hand of providence was in it all, and her mind, though fancy free, wandered nowhere but just according to the will of God, to effect the divine purpose. Pilate must be warned, so that his sentence may be his own act and deed, and that warning is given him through his wife's dream. So doth Providence work.

Note, next, the providence of God in arranging that *with this dream there should be great mental suffering.* "I have suffered many things in a dream concerning him!" I cannot tell what vision passed before her mind's eye, but it was one which caused her terrible agony. A modern artist has painted a picture of what he imagined the dream to be, but I shall not attempt to follow that great man in the exercise of fancy. Pilate's wife may have realized in her sleep the dreadful spectacle of the thorn-crown and the scourge, or even of the crucifixion and the death-agony; and truly I know of nothing more calculated to make the heart suffer many things concerning the Lord Jesus than a glance at His death. Around the cross there gathers grief enough to cause many a sleepless night, if the soul has any tenderness left in it.

Or her dream may have been of quite another kind. She may have seen in vision the Just One coming in the clouds of heaven. Her mind may have pictured Him upon the great white throne, even the Man Whom her husband was about to condemn to die. She may have seen her husband brought forth to judgment, himself a prisoner to be tried by the Just One, who had aforetime been accused before him. She may have awoke, startled at the shriek of her husband as he fell back into the pit that knows no bottom. Whatever it was, she had suffered repeated painful emotions in the dream, and she awoke startled and amazed. The terror of the night was upon her, and it threatened to become a terror to her for all her days, and she therefore hastens to stay her husband's hand.

Now, herein is the hand of God, and the simple story goes to prove that the wandering Zingari of dreamland are still under His control, and He can cause them to produce distress and anguish, if some grand end is to be served thereby.

Equally remarkable is it that *she should have sent to her husband the message*, "Have nothing to do with this just person." Most dreams we quite forget; a few we mention as remarkable, and only now and then one is impressed upon us so that we remember it for years. Scarcely have any of you had a dream which made you send a message to a magistrate upon the bench. Such an intention would only be resorted to in an urgent case. Though the judge were your own husband you would be very hard pressed before you would worry him with your dreams while he was occupied with important public business. Mostly a dream may wait till business is over. But so deep was the impression upon this Roman lady's mind that she does not wait until her lord comes home, but sends to him at once. Her advice is urgent —"Have thou nothing to do with this Just One." She must warn him now, before he has laid a stroke on Him, much less imbrued his hands in His blood. Not "have a little to do and scourge Him, and let Him go," but "have thou nothing to do with Him. Say not an unkind word, nor do Him any injury! Deliver Him from His adversaries! If He must die, let it be by some other hand than thine! My husband, my husband, my husband, I beseech thee, have thou nothing to do with this just Person. Let Him alone, I pray thee!" She words her message very emphatically. It shows a wonderful providence of God that this lady was moved to send so strong a message to her self-willed husband, to beseech, to entreat, to implore, almost to demand of him, that he let this just Man go. O Providence, how mightily canst thou work! O Lord, the seraphim obey Thee, but Thou findest an equally willing servitor in a wife who, at Thy bidding, stands between her husband and a crime.

Once more, about this providence I want you to notice *the peculiar time in which her warning came*. It was evidently a dream of the morning: "I have suffered many things in a dream this day." The day had not long broken—it was yet early in the morning. The Romans had a superstition that morning dreams are true. I suppose it was after her husband had left her that she thus dreamed. If I may be allowed, not to state a fact, but to make a conjecture, which seems to me most probable, she was a dearly beloved wife, but sickly, and therefore needed to rest further into the day than her husband; and when he had left his couch she had yet another sleep, and being a sensitive person, and all the more likely to dream, she awoke from her morning sleep oppressed with a terror which she could not shake off. Pilate was gone, and she was told that he was in the judgment-hall. She asked her attendants why he was there so early, and they replied that there had been an unusual clamour in the courtyard, for the high priests and a mob of Jews had been there, and the governor had gone out to them. They might, perhaps, also tell her that Jesus of Nazareth was brought there a prisoner, and the priests were entreating Pilate to put Him to death, though they had heard the governor say that he found no fault in Him.

"Go," she said to her maid, "call to one of the guards and bid him go at once to my husband, and say what I tell you. Let him speak aloud, that some of the cruel Jews may hear it, and be moved from their cruel purpose: let him say that I implore my husband to have nothing to do with this just Person, for I have suffered many things this very morning in a dream concerning Him." The warning came at the nick of time, as we say, though, alas, it came in vain! Admire the punctuality of Providence. God never is before His time; He never is too late. It shall be seen concerning all that He doeth that on the selfsame day determined by the prophecy the fulfilment came. My soul stands trembling while she sings the glory of her God, whose providence is high, even like Ezekiel's wheels; but the wheels are full of eyes, and, as they turn, all the surroundings are observed and provided for, so that there are no slips, or oversights, or accidents, or delays. Prompt and effectual is the operation of the Lord.

Thus much concerning Providence, and I think you will all agree that my point is proven—that providence is always co-working with the grace of God. A great writer who knows but little about divine things, yet, nevertheless, tells us that he perceives a power in the world which works for righteousness. Exactly so! It is well spoken, for this is the chief of all powers. When you and I go out to warn men of sin, we are not alone, all Providence is at our back. When we preach Christ crucified, we are workers together with God; God is working with us as well as by us. Everything that happens is driving towards the end for which we work, when we seek to convince men of sin and of righteousness.

Where the Spirit of God is, all the forces of nature and providence are mustered. The fall of empires, the death of despots, the uprise of nations, the making or the breaking of treaties, terrific wars and blighting famines, are all working out the grand end. Yea, and domestic matters, such as the death of children, the sickness of wives, the loss of work, the poverty of the family, and a thousand other things are working, working, ever working, for the improvement of men; and you and I, lending our poor feebleness to co-operate with God, are marching with all the forces of the universe. Have comfort, then, in this. O workers for Jesus, suffering many things for Him, be of good courage, for the stars in their courses fight for the servants of the living God, and the stones of the field are in league with you.

II. Secondly, I gather from this story THE ACCESSIBILITY OF CONSCIENCE TO GOD. How are we to reach Pilate? How are we to give him warning? He has rejected the voice of Jesus and the sight of Jesus—could not Peter be fetched to expostulate with him? Alas, he has denied his Master. Could not John be brought in? Even he has forsaken the Lord. Where shall a messenger be found? It shall be found in a dream. God can get at men's hearts, however hardened they may be. Never give them up, never despair of arousing them. If my ministry, your ministry, and the ministry of the blessed Book should all seem to be nothing, God can reach the conscience by a dream. If the sword cometh not at them at close quarters, yet what seems but a stray arrow from a bow drawn at a venture shall find out the joints in their harness. We ought to believe in God about wicked men, and never say of them, "It is impossible that they should be converted." The Lord can wound leviathan, for His weapons are many, and they are suited to the foe. I do not think a dream would operate upon *my* mind to convince me; but certain minds lie open in that direction, and to them a dream may be a power. God may use even superstition to accomplish His beneficent purposes. Many besides Pilate have been warned by dreams.

Better still, Pilate was accessible through the dream *of his wife*. Henry Melvill has a very wonderful discourse upon this topic, in which he tries to show that probably if Pilate had dreamed this dream himself it would not have been so operative upon him as when his wife dreamed it. He takes it as a supposition, which nobody can deny, that Pilate had an affectionate and tender wife, who was very dear to him. The one brief narrative which we have of her certainly looks that way; it is evident that she loved her husband dearly, and would therefore prevent his acting unjustly to Jesus. To send a warning by her was to reach Pilate's conscience through his affections.

If his beloved wife was distressed it would be sure to weigh heavily with him: for he would not have her troubled. He would fain shield his tender one from every breath of wind and give her perfect comfort, and when she pleads it is his delight to yield: it is, therefore, no small trouble to him that she is suffering, suffering so much as to send a message to him,

suffering because of One Who deserves her good opinion—One
Whom he himself knows to be without fault. If this lady was
indeed the wife of Pilate's youth, tender and dearly beloved,
and if she was gradually sickening before his eyes, her pale
face would rise before his loving memory, and her words would
have boundless power over him when she said, "I have suffered
many things in a dream." O Claudia Procula, if that were
thy name, well did the Lord of mercy entrust His message to
thy persuasive lips, for from thee it would come with tenfold
influence.

Tradition declares this lady to have been a Christian, and
the Greek church have placed her in their calendar as a saint.
For this we have no evidence; all that we know is that she was
Pilate's wife, and used her wifely influence to stay him from
this crime. How often has a tender, suffering, loving woman
exercised great power over a coarse, rough man! The All-wise
One knows this, and hence He often speaks to sinful men by
this influential agency. He converts one in a family that she
may be His missionary to the rest. Thus He speaks with something better than the tongues of men and of angels, for He uses
love itself to be His orator. Affection has more might than
eloquence. That is why, my friend, God sent you for a little
while that dear child who prattled to you about the Saviour.
She is gone to heaven now, but the music of her little hymns
rings in your ear even now, and her talk about Jesus and the
angels is yet with you. She has been called home; but God
sent her to you for a season to charm you to Himself and win
you to the right way. Thus he bade you cease from sin and
turn to Christ.

And that dear mother of yours, who is now before the throne,
do you remember what she said to you when she was dying?
You have heard me a great many times, but you never heard
a sermon from me like that address from her dying couch.
You can never quite forget it, or shake yourself free from its
power. Beware how you trifle with it. To Pilate his wife's message
was God's ultimatum; He warned him never again, and even
Jesus stood silent before him. The selection of the wife was
no doubt made by infinite wisdom and tenderness, that if
possible Pilate might be arrested in his career of crime and
strengthened to the performance of an act of justice by which
he would have avoided the most terrible of crimes.

So, then, we may safely conclude that the Lord has His
missionaries where the city missionary cannot enter; He sends
the little children to sing and pray where the preacher is never
heard; He moves the godly woman to proclaim the gospel by
her lip and life where the Bible is not read. He sends a sweet

girl to grow up and win a brother or a father where no other voice would be allowed to tell of Jesus and His love. We thank God it is so; it gives hope for the households of this godless city,—it gives us hope even for those for whom the Sabbath-bell rings out in vain. They will hear, they must hear these home preachers, these messengers who tug at their hearts.

Ay, and let me add that where God does not employ a dream, nor use a wife, yet he can get at men's conscience by no visible means but *by thoughts which come unbidden and abide upon the soul*. Truths long buried suddenly rise up, and when the man is in the very act of sin he is stopped in the way, as Balaam was when the angel met him. Brothers and sisters, use for the good of men anything which comes in your way. Use not only sober argument and sound doctrine, but even if a dream has touched your heart, do not hesitate to repeat it where it may have effect. Any weapon may be used in this war. But see to it that you do seek the souls of men, all of you. You who are wives should be especially stirred up to this sacred work. Never keep back from an ungodly husband the word which may convert him from the error of his ways. And you, dear children, you sisters, you of the gentler sort, do not hesitate, in your own quiet way, to be heralds for Jesus wherever your lot is cast. As for us all, let us take care that we use every occasion for repressing sin and creating holiness. Let us warn the ungodly at once; for perhaps the man to whom we are sent has not yet performed the fatal deed. Let us stand in the gap while yet there is space for repentance.

That is our second point. God bless it; although I cannot preach upon it as I would, the Spirit of God can put power into it.

III. Thirdly, we have now the lamentable task of observing THE FREQUENT FAILURE EVEN OF THE BEST MEANS. I have ventured to say that, humanly speaking, it was the best means of reaching Pilate's conscience for his wife to be led to expostulate with him. He would hear but few, but her he would hear; and yet even her warning was in vain. What was the reason?

First, *self-interest* was involved in the matter, and that is a powerful factor. Pilate was afraid of losing his governorship. The Jews would be angry if he did not obey their cruel bidding; they might complain to Tiberius, and he would lose his lucrative position. Alas, such things as these are holding some of you captives to sin at this moment. You cannot afford to be true and right, for it would cost too much. You know the will of the Lord; you know what is right; but you renounce Christ by putting Him off, and by abiding in the ways of sin that you may gain the wages thereof. You are afraid that to be a true

Christian would involve the loss of a friend's goodwill, or the patronage of an ungodly person, or the smile of an influential worldling, and this you cannot afford. You count the cost, and reckon that it is too high. You resolve to gain the world, even though you lose your soul! What then? You will go to hell rich! A sorry result this! Do you see anything desirable in such an attainment? Oh that you would consider your ways and listen to the voice of wisdom!

The next reason why his wife's appeal was ineffectual was the fact that Pilate was *a coward*. A man with legions at his back, and yet afraid of a Jewish mob—afraid to let one poor prisoner go whom he knew to be innocent; afraid because he knew his conduct would not bear inspection! He was, morally, a coward! Multitudes of people go to hell because they have not the courage to fight their way to heaven. "The fearful and unbelieving shall have their portion in the lake which burneth with fire and brimstone, which is the second death." So saith the word of God. They are afraid of encountering a fool's laugh, and so rush upon everlasting contempt. They could not bear to tear themselves away from old companions, and excite remarks and sarcasm among ungodly wits, and so they keep their companions and perish with them. They have not the pluck to say "No," and swim against the stream; they are such cowardly creatures that they will sooner be for ever lost than face a little scorn.

Yet while there was cowardice in Pilate, there was *presumption* too. He who was afraid of man and afraid to do right, yet dared to incur the guilt of innocent blood. Oh, the cowardice of Pilate to take water and wash his hands, as if he could wash off blood with water; and then to say, "I am innocent of his blood"—which was a lie—"see ye to it." By those last words he brought the blood upon himself, for he consigned his Prisoner to their tender mercies, and they could not have laid a hand upon Him unless he had given them leave. Oh, the daring of Pilate thus in the sight of God to commit murder and disclaim it. There is a strange mingling of cowardliness and courage about many men; they are afraid of a man, but not afraid of the eternal God who can destroy both body and soul in hell. This is why men are not saved, even when the best of means are used, because they are presumptuous, and dare defy the Lord.

Besides this, Pilate was *double-minded*: he had a heart and a heart. He had a heart after that which was right, for he sought to release Jesus; but he had another heart after that which was gainful, for he would not run the risk of losing his post by incurring the displeasure of the Jews. We have plenty around us who are double-minded. Such are here this morning; but where were they last night? You will be touched by to-day's sermon! How will you be affected to-morrow by a lewd speech or a lascivious song? Many men run two ways; they seem earnest about their souls, but they are far more eager after gain or pleasure. They dare not run risks, and yet, meanwhile, they run the awful risk of being driven for ever from the presence of God to the place where hope can never come. Oh that my words were shot as from a culverin! Oh that they would hurl a cannon-shot at indecision! Oh that I could speak like God's own thunder, which maketh the hinds to calve, and breaketh the rocks in pieces: even so would I warn men against these desperate evils which thwart the efforts of mercy, so that, even when the man's own wife, with tenderest love, bids him escape from the wrath to come, he still chooses his own destruction.

IV. Lastly, we have a point which is yet more terrible, THE OVERWHELMING CONDEMNATION OF THOSE WHO THUS TRANSGRESS. This Pilate was guilty beyond all excuse. He deliberately and of his own free will condemned the just Son of God to die, being informed that He was the Son of God, and knowing both from his own examination and from his wife that He was a "just Person."

Observe that the message which he received was most distinct. It was suggested by a dream; but there is nothing dreamy about it. It is as plain as words can be put:—"Have thou nothing to do with that just man: for I have suffered many things this day in a dream because of him." He condemned the Lord with his eyes open, and that is an awful way of sinning. Oh, my dear friends, am I addressing any here who are purposing to do some very sinful thing, but have lately received a warning from God? I would add one more caution. I pray you by the blessed God, and by the bleeding Saviour, and as you love yourself, and as you love her from whom the warning may have come to you, do stop, and hold your hand! Do not this abominable thing! You know better. The warning is not put to you in some mysterious and obscure way; but it comes point blank to you in unmistakable terms. God has sent conscience to you, and He has enlightened that conscience, so that it speaks very plain English to you. This morning's discourse stops you on the highway of sin, puts its pistol to your ear, and demands that you "Stand and deliver." Stir an inch, and it will be at your own soul's peril. Do you hear me? Will you regard the heaven-sent expostulation? Oh, that you would stand still awhile and hear what God shall speak while He bids you yield yourself to Christ to-day. It may be *now or never* with you, as it was with Pilate that day.

Beside that, Pilate was sinning not only after distinct warning, and a warning which set out the blackness of the sin, but he was sinning after his conscience had been touched and moved through his affections. It is a dreadful thing to sin against a mother's prayer. She stands in your way; she stretches out her arms, with tears she declares that she will block your road to perdition. Will you force your way to ruin over her prostrate form? She kneels! She grasps your knees, she begs you not to be lost. Are you so brutal as to trample on her love? Your little child entreats you; will you disregard her tears? Alas, she was yours, but death has removed her, and ere she departed she entreated you to follow her to heaven and she sang her little hymn—

"Yes, we'll gather at the river."

Will you fling your babe aside as though you were another Herod that would slay the innocents, and all in order that you may curse yourself for ever and be your own destroyer? It is hard for me to talk to you thus. If it is coming home to any of you it will be very hard for you to hear it; indeed, I hope it will be so hard that you will end it by saying, "I will yield to love which assails me by such tender entreaties."

It will not be a piece of mere imagination if I conceive that at the last great day, when Jesus sits upon the judgment-seat, and Pilate stands there to be judged for the deeds done in the body, that his wife will be a swift witness against him to condemn him. I can imagine that at the last great day there will be many such scenes as that, wherein those who loved us best will bring the most weighty evidences against us, if we are still in our sins. I know how it affected me as a lad when my mother, after setting before her children the way of salvation, said to us, "If you refuse Christ and perish, I cannot plead in your favour and say that you were ignorant. No, but I must say Amen to your condemnation." I could not bear *that*! Would my mother say "Amen" to my condemnation? And yet, Pilate's wife, what canst thou do otherwise? When all must speak the truth, what canst thou say but that thy husband was tenderly and earnestly warned by thee and yet consigned the Saviour to His enemies?

Oh, my ungodly hearers, my soul goes out after you. "Turn ye, turn ye, why will ye die?" Why will ye sin against the Saviour? God grant you may not reject your own salvation, but may turn to Christ and find eternal redemption in Him. "Whosoever believeth in him hath everlasting life."

SILVER SOCKETS: OR, REDEMPTION THE FOUNDATION

A SERMON

Text.—"And the Lord spake unto Moses, saying, When thou takest the sum of the children of Israel after their number, then shall they give every man a ransom for his soul unto the Lord, when thou numberest them; that there be no plague among them, when thou numberest them. This they shall give, every one that passeth among them that are numbered, half a shekel after the shekel of the sanctuary (a shekel is twenty gerahs): an half shekel shall be the offering of the Lord. Every one that passeth among them that are numbered, from twenty years old and above, shall give an offering unto the Lord. The rich shall not give more, and the poor shall not give less than half a shekel, when they give an offering unto the Lord, to make an atonement for your souls. And thou shalt take the atonement money of the children of Israel, and shalt appoint it for the service of the tabernacle of the congregation; that it may be a memorial unto the children of Israel before the Lord, to make an atonement for your souls."—Exodus xxx. 11–16.

"A bekah for every man, that is, half a shekel, after the shekel of the sanctuary, for every one that went to be numbered, from twenty years old and upward, for six hundred thousand and three thousand and five hundred and fifty men. And of the hundred talents of silver were cast the sockets of the sanctuary, and the sockets of the vail; an hundred sockets of the hundred talents, a talent for a socket." —Exodus xxxviii. 26–27.

WILL you kindly first open your Bibles at Exodus xxx.; for I must commence my discourse by expounding that passage. When the account was taken of the number of the children of Israel the Lord commanded that every male over twenty years of age should pay half a shekel as redemption money, confessing that he deserved to die, owning that he was in debt to God, and bringing the sum demanded as a type of a great redemption which would by-and-by be paid for the souls of the sons of men.

The truth was thus taught that God's people are a redeemed people: they are elsewhere called "the redeemed of the Lord." If men reject the redemption which He ordains, then are they not His people; for all His chosen it may be said—"The Lord hath redeemed Jacob, and ransomed him from the hand of him that was stronger than he." Whenever we attempt to number up the people of God it is absolutely needful that we count only those who at least profess to have brought the redemption price in their hands, and so to have taken part in the atonement of Christ Jesus. David, when he numbered the people, did not gather from them the redemption money, and hence a plague broke out amongst them. He had failed in obedience to the Lord's ordinance, and counted his subjects, not as redeemed people, but merely as so many heads.

Let us always beware of estimating the number of Christians by the number of the population of the countries called Christian; for the only true Christians in the world are those who are redeemed from iniquity by the blood of the Lamb, and have personally accepted the ransom which the Lord has provided, personally brought their redemption money in their hands by taking Christ to be theirs and presenting Him by an act of faith to the great Father. God has upon earth as many people as believe in Jesus Christ, and we dare not count any others to be His but those who can say, "In whom we have redemption through his blood, the forgiveness of sins." We must not count heads which know about Christ, but hands which have received the redemption money and are presenting it unto God; not so much persons who are called Christians by courtesy as souls that are Christly in very fact, because they have accepted the atoning sacrifice, and live before God as "redeemed from among men."

Observe that this redemption, without which no man might rightly be numbered among the children of Israel lest a plague should break out among them, must be *personal and individual*. There was not a lump sum to be paid for the nation, or twelve amounts for the twelve tribes; but each man must bring his own half shekel for himself. So there is no redemption that will be of any use to any of you unless it is personally accepted and brought before God by faith. You must each one be able to say for yourself concerning the Lord Jesus, "He loved me, and gave himself for me."

It was *absolutely essential* that each one should bring the half shekel of redemption money; for redemption is the only way in which you and I can be accepted of God. If birth could have done it, they had the privilege beyond all doubt; for they had Abraham to their father: they were lineally descended from the three great patriarchs, and they might have said, "We be Abraham's seed, and were never in bondage to any man." Nay, but salvation is not of blood, nor of birth, nor of the will of the flesh: salvation is by redemption, and even the true child of Abraham must bring his redemption money. So must you, you child of godly parents, find salvation by the redemption which is in Christ Jesus, or be lost for ever. Do not believe the falsehood of certain modern divines, that you children of godly

parents do not need to be converted because you are born so
nobly and brought up so tenderly by your parents. You are
by nature heirs of wrath even as others. "Ye must be born
again," and ye must be personally redeemed as well as heathen
children, or else you will perish, though the blood of ministers,
martyrs, and apostles should be running in your veins. Redemption is the only ground of acceptance before God, and
not godly birth, or pious education.

There were many, no doubt, in the camp of Israel who were
men of station and substance; but *they* must bring the ransom
money, or die amid their wealth. Others were wise-hearted and
skilful in the arts, yet must they be redeemed or die. Rank could
not save the princes, nor office spare the elders: every man of
Israel must be redeemed; and no man could pass the muster-
roll without his half shekel, whatever he might say, or do, or
be. God was their God because He had redeemed them out
of the house of bondage, and they were His people because He
had "put a redemption between his people and the Egyptians."
Well did David ask, "What one nation in the earth is like thy
people, even like Israel, whom God went to redeem for a people
to himself?"

Note well that every Israelitish man must be *alike redeemed*
and redeemed with the like, nay, with the same redemption.
"The rich shall not give more, and the poor shall not give less
than half a shekel." Every man requires redemption, the one
as well as the other. Kings on their thrones must be redeemed
as well as prisoners in their dungeons; the philosopher must be
redeemed as well as the peasant; the preacher as much as the
profligate, and the moralist as certainly as the prostitute or the
thief. The redemption money for every person must be the same,
for all have sinned and are in like condemnation.

And it must be *a redemption that meets the divine demand*, because,
you see, the Lord not only says that they must each bring half
a shekel, no more, no less, but it must be "the shekel of the
sanctuary,"—not the shekel of commerce, which might be de-
based in quality or diminished by wear and tear, but the coin
must be according to the standard shekel laid up in the holy
place. To make sure of it Moses defines exactly how much a
shekel was worth, and what its weight was,—"A shekel is twenty
gerahs." So you must bring to God the redemption which He
has appointed,—the blood and righteousness of Christ,—nothing
more, nothing less. The ransom of Christ is perfection, and
from it there must be no varying. The price must satisfy the
Divine demand, and that to the full.

Now we turn to the second of our texts, and there we learn
a very remarkable fact. In the thirty-eighth chapter, verse

twenty-five, we find that this mass of silver which was paid, whereby six hundred and three thousand five hundred and fifty men were redeemed, each one paying his half shekel, came to a great weight of silver. It must have weighed something over four tons, and this was dedicated to the use of the tabernacle: the special application of the precious metal was to make sockets into which the boards which made the walls of the tabernacle should be placed. The mass of silver made up one hundred talents, and these unheld the fifty boards of the holy place. They were in a wilderness, constantly moving, and continually shifting the tabernacle. Now, they might have dug out a foundation in the sand, or on coming to a piece of rock where they could not dig, they might have cut out foundations with great toil; but the Lord appointed that they should carry the foundation of the tabernacle with them.

A talent of silver, weighing, I suppose, close upon one hundred pounds, was either formed into the shape of a wedge, so as to be driven into the soil, or else made into a solid square plate to lie upon it. In the wedge or plate were made mortises, into which the tenons of the boards could be readily fitted. These plates of silver fitted the one into the other, tenon and mortise wise, and thus they made a compact parallelogram, strengthened at the corners with double plates, and formed one foundation, moveable when taken to pieces, yet very secure as a whole. *This foundation was made of the redemption money.*

See the instructive emblem! The foundation of the worship of Israel was redemption. The dwelling-place of the Lord their God was founded on atonement. All the boards of incorruptible wood and precious gold stood upon the redemption price, and the curtains of fine linen, and the veil of matchless workmanship, and the whole structure rested on nothing else but the solid mass of silver which had been paid as the redemption money of the people. There was only one exception, and that was at the door where was the entrance to the holy place. There the pillars were set upon sockets of brass, perhaps because, as there was much going in and out of the priests, it was not meet that they should tread upon the token of redemption. The blood of the paschal Lamb, when Israel came out of Egypt, was sprinkled on the lintel and the two side posts; but out of reverence to that blood it was not to be sprinkled on the threshold. Everything was done to show that atonement is to be the precious foundation of all holy things, and everything to prevent a slighting or disregard of it. Woe unto that man of whom it shall ever be said, "He hath trodden under foot the Son of God, and hath counted the blood of the covenant, wherewith he was sanctified, an unholy thing."

Moreover, this does not stand alone; for when the Tabernacle was succeeded by the Temple redemption was still conspicuous in the foundation. What was the foundation of the Temple? It was the rock of Mount Moriah. And what was the hill of Moriah but the place where in many lights redemption and atonement had been set forth. It was there that Abraham drew the knife to slay Isaac: a fair picture of the Father offering up His Son. It was there the ram was caught in the thicket and was killed instead of Isaac: fit emblem of the substitute accepted instead of man. Later still, it was on Mount Moriah that the angel, when David attempted to number the people without redemption money, stood with his sword drawn. There David offered sacrifices and burnt offerings. The offering was accepted and the angel sheathed his sword—another picture of that power of redemption by which mercy rejoices against judgment. And there the Lord uttered the memorable sentence, "It is enough, stay now thine hand."

This "enough" is the crown of redemption. Even as the Great Sacrifice Himself said, "It is finished," so does the Great Accepter of the sacrifice say, "enough." What a place of redemption was the hill of Zion! Now, if the temple was built on a mount which must have been especially selected because there the types of redemption were most plentiful, I feel that without an apology I may boldly take this first fact that the building of the tabernacle in the wilderness was based and grounded upon redemption money, and use it for our instruction.

I. First, I want you to view this illustration as teaching us something about GOD IN RELATION TO MAN. The tent in the wilderness was typical of God's coming down to man to hold intercourse with him: the fiery cloudy pillar visible outside, and the bright light of the shekinah, visible to him who was called to enter once a year into the innermost sanctuary, shining over the mercy-seat,—these were the tokens of the special presence of the Deity in the centre of the camp of Israel. The Lord seems to teach us, in relation to His dealing with men, that *He will meet man in the way of grace only on the footing of redemption.* He treats with man concerning love and grace within His holy shrine; but the basis of that shrine must be atonement. Rest assured, dear friends, that there is no meeting with God on our part except through Jesus Christ our Redeemer. I am of Luther's mind when he said, "I will have nothing to do with an absolute God." God out of Christ is a terror to us. Even in Christ, remember, He is a consuming fire, for even "Our God is a consuming fire"; but what He must be out of Christ may none of us ever know.

"Till God in human flesh I see,
  My thoughts no comfort find;
The holy, just, and sacred Three
  Are terrors to my mind.

"But if Immanuel's face appear,
  My hope, my joy begins;
His name forbids my slavish fear,
  His grace removes my sins."

Always enter the holy place with the thought, "I know that my Redeemer liveth." "Not without blood": recollect that! Into the holy place went the high priest once every year, "not without blood." There can be no coming of God to man on terms of peace except through the one great Sacrifice: that must be the foundation of it all.

Nay, and not only God's coming to us, but *God's abiding with us is upon the same foundation*; for the tabernacle was, so to speak, the house of God,—the place where God especially dwelt among His people, as He said: "I will dwell in them, and walk in them." But He never dwelt among them in anything but in a tent that was based upon the silver of the redemption money; and you, dear friend, if you have ever walked with God, can only maintain your fellowship by resting where you did at first, as a poor sinner redeemed by your Saviour. They have asked me to rise sometimes to a higher platform, and come to God as a sanctified person. Yes, but a rock, though it may be lower than the little wooden stage which some erect upon it, is safer to stand upon; and I do believe that those who walk with God, according to their attainments, and imaginary perfections, have climbed up to a rotten stage, which will fall under them ere long. I know no mode of standing before God to-day but that which I had at first. I am unworthy still in myself, but accepted in the Beloved! Guilty in myself, and lost and ruined; but still received, blessed, and loved, because of the person and work of Christ. The Lord cannot dwell with you, my dear friend, you will soon have broken fellowship and be in the dark, if you attempt to walk with Him because you feel sanctified, or because you have been active in His service, or because you know much, or because you are an experienced believer. No! no! no! The Lord will only abide with us in that tabernacle whose every board is resting upon the silver foundation of redemption by His own dear Son.

There can, beloved, be no sort of *communion* between God and us except through the atonement. Do you want to pray? You cannot speak with God except through Jesus Christ. Do you wish to praise? You cannot bring the censer full of smoking

incense except through Christ. It is only within those foundations of silver that you can speak to God, or hear Him speak
comfortably with you. Would you hear a voice out of the excellent glory? Do you pray that the great Father would speak with
you as with His dear children? Expect it through Jesus Christ,
for "through him we have access by one Spirit unto the Father."
Even unto the Father, though we be children, we have not
access except through Jesus. The tabernacle of communion even
to him that lives nearest to God must be built upon the redemption price. Free grace and dying love must be the golden bells
which ring upon our garments when we go into the holy place
to speak with the Most High.

The tabernacle was the place of *holy service*, where the priests
all day long offered sacrifices of one kind and another unto the
Most High. And you and I serve God as priests, for He has
made us a royal priesthood. But how and where can we exercise
our priesthood? Everywhere as to this world; but before God,
the foundation of the temple wherein we stand, and the ground
of the acceptance of our priesthood, is redemption. We must
bring our offerings unto that court which is fenced about by the
foundation most precious which God has laid of old, even the
merit of His dear Son. We are accepted in the Beloved, and in
no other manner; we are shut in within the foundation which
Christ has laid of old, not with corruptible things as with silver
and gold, but with His own most precious blood.

II. I think we may, in the second place, apply this illustration
to CHRIST IN HIS DIVINE PERSON. The Tabernacle was the type
of our Lord Jesus Christ, for God dwells among men in Christ.
"He tabernacled among us, and we beheld his glory," says the
apostle. God dwelleth not in temples made with hands, that is
to say, of this building; but the Temple of God is Christ Jesus
"in whom dwelleth all the fulness of the Godhead bodily."

Our Lord is thus the Tabernacle which the Lord hath pitched
and not man; and *our first and fundamental idea of Him must be in
His character as Redeemer.* Our Lord does come to us in other
characters, and in them all He is right glorious; but unless we
receive Him as Redeemer we have missed the essence of His
character, the foundation idea of Him. As the tent in the wilderness was founded upon the redemption money, so our idea and
conception of Christ must be first of all that "he is the propitiation for our sins"; and I say this, though it may seem unnecessary to say it, because Satan is very crafty, and he leads many
from plain truth by subtle means.

I remember a sister, who had been a member of a certain
denomination, who was converted to God in this place, though
she had been a professed Christian for years. She said to me,

"I have hitherto believed only in Christ crucified: I worshipped Him as about to come in the second Advent to reign with His people, but I never had a sense of guilt, neither did I go to Him as putting away my sin; and hence I was not saved." When she began to see herself as a sinner she found her need of a Redeemer. Atonement must enter into our first and chief idea of the Lord Jesus. "We preach Christ *crucified*": we preach Him glorified, and delight to do so; but still the main point upon which the eye of a sinner must rest, if he would have peace with God, must be Christ crucified for sin. "God forbid that I should glory save in the cross of our Lord Jesus Christ."

Do, then, my dear hearer, let the very foundation of your faith in Christ be your view of Him as ransoming you from the power of sin and Satan. Some say they admire Christ as an example, and well say they may; they can never find a better: but Jesus Christ will never be truly known and followed if He be viewed only as an example, for He is infinitely more than that. Neither can any man carry out the project of being like Christ, unless he first knows Him as making atonement for sin, and as giving power to overcome sin through His blood.

Let this then be your basic idea of Christ—"he has redeemed us from the curse of the law." Indeed, in reference to Christ, we must regard His redemption as the basis of His triumphs and His glory—"the sufferings of Christ and the glory that shall follow." We cannot understand any work that He has performed unless we understand His vicarious sacrifice. Christ is a lock without a key, He is a labyrinth without a clue, until you know Him as the Redeemer. You have spilt the letters on the floor, and you cannot make out the character of the Wonderful till first you have learned to spell the words—atonement by blood. This is the deepest joy of earth and the grandest song in heaven. "For thou wast slain, and hast redeemed us unto God by thy blood."

I beg you to observe, in connection with our text, that as the foundation of the Tabernacle was very valuable, so our Lord Jesus as our Redeemer is *exceedingly precious to us*. His redemption is made with His precious blood. The redemption money was of pure and precious metal, a metal that does not lose weight in the fire. "The redemption of the soul is precious." What a redemption price hath Christ given for us; yea, what a redemption price He is! Well did Peter say, "Unto you that believe he is precious"; silver and gold are not to be mentioned in comparison with Him.

To me it is very instructive that the Israelites should have been redeemed with silver in the form of half-shekels, because there are many who say, "These old-fashioned divines believe in the mercantile idea of the atonement." Exactly so: we always did and always shall use a metaphor which is so expressive as to be abhorred by the enemies of the truth. The mercantile idea of the atonement is the Biblical idea of the atonement. These people were redeemed, not with lumps of uncoined silver, but with money used in commerce. Paul saith "Ye are not your own: ye are bought"—listen—"*with a price*"—to give us the mercantile idea beyond all question. "Bought with a price" is doubly mercantile. What say you to this, ye wise refiners, who would refine the meaning out of the. word of the Lord? Such persons merely use this expression about the "mercantile idea" as a cheap piece of mockery, because in their hearts they hate atonement altogether, and the idea of substitution and expiation by vicarious sacrifice is abhorrent to them. Therefore hath the Lord made it so plain, so manifest that they may stumble at this stumbling-stone, "whereunto also," methinks, as Peter saith, "they were appointed." To us, at any rate, the redemption price which is the foundation of all is exceedingly precious.

But there is one other thing to recollect in reference to Christ, namely, that *we must each one view Him as our own*, for out of all the grown up males that were in the camp of Israel, when they set up the tabernacle, there was not one but had a share in its foundation. We read in Exodus xxxv. 25 and 26, "And all the women that were wise hearted did spin with their hands, and brought that which they had spun, both of blue, and of purple, and of scarlet, and of fine linen. And all the women whose hearts stirred them up in wisdom spun goats' hair." The men could not spin, perhaps; they did not understand that art; but every man had his half a shekel in the foundation. I want you to think of that. Each believer has a share in Christ as his redemption: nay, I dare not say a share in Him, for He is all mine, and He is all yours.

Brother and sister, have you by faith laid hold upon a whole Christ and said, "He has paid the price for me?" Then you have an interest in the very fundamental idea of Christ. Perhaps you are not learned enough to have enjoyed your portion in certain other aspects of our Lord; but if you are a believer, however weak you are, though you are like the poor among the people of Israel, you have your half shekel in the foundation. I delight to think of that. I have my treasure in Christ; "my Beloved is mine." Do you say He is yours? I do not deny it. So He is, but "He is mine." If you deny that fact we will quarrel at once, for I do aver that "my Beloved is mine." Moreover, by His purchase "I am His." "So am I," say you. Quite right: I am glad you are; but I know that "I am His." There is nothing like getting a firm, personal hold and grip of Christ: my half shekel is in the basis of the tabernacle; my redemption money is in the divinely glorious building of grace; my redemption is in the death of Christ, which is the foundation of all.

III. Time fails me, and yet I have now a third thought to lay before you very briefly. The tabernacle was a type of THE CHURCH OF GOD as the place of divine indwelling. What and where is the church of God? The true church is founded upon redemption. Every board of shittim wood was tenoned and mortised into the sockets of silver made of the redemption money, and every man that is in the church of God is united to Christ, rests upon Christ, and cannot be separated from Him. If that is not true of you, my dear hearer, you are not in the church of God. You may be in the Church of England or of Rome, you may be in this church or some other; but unless you are joined to Christ, and He is the sole foundation upon which you rest, you are not in the church of God. You may be in no visible church whatever, and yet, if you are resting upon Christ, you are a part of the true house of God on earth.

Christ is *a sure foundation for the church*; for the tabernacle was never blown down. It had no foundation but the talents of silver; and yet it braved every desert storm. The wilderness is a place of rough winds—it is called a howling wilderness; but the sockets of silver held the boards upright, and the holy tents defied the rage of the elements. To be united to Christ by faith is to be built on a sure foundation. His church will never be overthrown let the devil send what hurricanes he may.

And it was *an invariable foundation*, for the tabernacle always had the same basis wherever it was placed. One day it was pitched on the sand, another on a good piece of arable ground, a third time on a grass plot, and to-morrow on a bare rock; but it always had the same foundation. The bearers of the holy furniture never left the silver sockets behind. Those four tons of silver were carried in their waggons, and put out first as the one and only foundation of the holy place. We are told that this is too sensible a century to need or accept the same gospel as the first, second, and third centuries. Yet these were the centuries of martyrs, the centuries of heroes, the centuries that conquered all the gods of Greece and Rome, the centuries of holy glory, and all this because they were the centuries of the gospel; but now we are so enlightened that our ears ache for something fresh, and under the influence of another gospel, which is not another, our beliefs are dwindling down from alps to anthills, and we ourselves from giants to pigmies.

You will want a microscope soon to see Christian faith in the land, it is getting to be so small and scarce. By God's grace some of us abide by the ark of the covenant, and mean to preach the same gospel which the saints received at the first. We shall imitate those who, having had a silver foundation at the first had a silver foundation for the tabernacle, even till they came to the promised land. It is a foundation that we dare not change. It must be the same, world without end, for Jesus Christ is the same yesterday, to-day, and for ever.

IV. Fourthly, and lastly, I think this tabernacle in the wilderness may be viewed as a type of THE GOSPEL, for the gospel is the revelation of God to man. The tent in the wilderness was the gospel according to Moses. Now, as that old gospel in the wilderness was, such must ours be, and I want to say just two or three things very plainly, and have done.

Redemption, atonement in the mercantile idea, must be *the foundation of our theology—doctrinal, practical, and experimental.* As to doctrine, they say a fish stinks first at the head, and men first go astray in their brains. When once there is anything wrong in your belief as to redemption you are wrong all through. I believe in the old rhyme—

> "What think you of Christ? is the test
>   To try both your state and your scheme,
> You cannot be right in the rest
>   Unless you think rightly of HIM."

If you get wrong on atonement you have turned a switch which will run the whole train of your thoughts upon the wrong line. You must know Christ as the Redeemer of His people, and their substitute, or your teaching will give an uncertain sound. As redemption must be the foundation of doctrinal divinity, so it must of practical divinity. "Ye are not your own: ye are bought with a price," must be the source of holiness, and the reason for consecration. The man that does not feel himself to be specially "redeemed from among men" will see no reason for being different from other men. "Christ loved his Church and gave himself *for it*"; he who sees no special giving of Christ for His Church will see no special reason why the Church should give herself to Christ.

Certainly redemption must be the foundation of experimental theology; for what is an experience worth that does not make us every day prize more and more the redeeming blood? The only gospel that I have to preach is that which I rest upon myself:—"Who his own self bare our sins in his own body on the tree"; "For the chastisement of our peace was upon him, and with his stripes we are healed"; "He bare the sin of many, and made intercession for the transgressors." Oh, dear hearers, build on that and you will never fail; but if you do not take Christ's redemption as the foundation of your hope—I do not

care who you are—you may be very learned, but you know
nothing at all. The Lord make you to know that you know
nothing, and then you will know something: and when you have
learned as much as that, may He teach you the redemption of
His Son, and reveal Christ in you.

This, beloved, is henceforth *the burden of our service, and the
glory of our life*. Those silver sockets were very precious, but
very weighty. I dare say the men who had to move them sometimes thought so. Four tons and more of silver make up a great
load. O blessed, blissful draught, to have to put the shoulder
to the collar to draw the burden of the Lord—the glorious weight
of redemption. My soul, blessed art thou to be made a labouring
ox for Christ; ever to be bearing among this people the divinely
precious load of the foundation which Christ has laid for His
people. You, young brethren, that preach, mind you always
carry your four tons of silver: preach a full and rich redemption
all of you. You who go to the Sunday School, do not let the
children have a place to live in that has no foundation: the first
wind will blow it over, and where will they be? Left naked
under the ruins of that in which they had hoped. Lay Christ
for a foundation. You cannot do better, for God Himself has
said, "Behold, I lay in Sion a chief corner stone, elect, precious."
Lay this silver foundation wherever you are.

Aye, but though the ingots were heavy to carry, every Israelite
felt proud to think that that tabernacle had a foundation of
silver. You Amalekites out there cannot see the silver footing
of it all; you Moabites cannot perceive it. All you can see is
the badger skins outside,—the rough exterior of the tent. You
say, "That tent is a poor place to be a temple: that gospel is
a very simple affair." No doubt it is to you, but you never saw
the silver sockets, you never saw the golden boards, you never
saw the glory of the inside of the place lit up by the seven-branched
candlesticks, and glorious with the presence of God. Brethren,
redemption is our honour and delight.

> "In the cross of Christ I glory
> Towering o'er the wrecks of time:
> All the light of sacred story
> Gathers round its head sublime."

This the first and this the last; the bleeding Lamb slain from
before the foundation of the world, and yet living and reigning
when earth's foundations shall dissolve. That blessed Lamb of
God is in the midst of the throne, and His people shall all be
with Him, for ever triumphant. He is the Alpha and Omega,
the beginning and the ending, the foundation and the headstone.
O Saviour of sinners, glory be to Thy name. Amen and amen.

THE GLORY OF GOD IN THE FACE OF
JESUS CHRIST

A Sermon

Text.—'For God, who commanded the light to shine out of darkness,
hath shined in our hearts, to give the light of the knowledge of the
glory of God in the face of Jesus Christ.''—2 Corinthians iv. 6.

THE apostle is explaining the reason for his preaching Christ
with so much earnestness: he had received divine light, and
he felt bound to spread it. One great motive power of a true
ministry is trusteeship. The Lord has put us in trust with the
gospel; He has filled us with a treasure with which we are to
enrich the world. The text explains in full what it is with which
the Lord has entrusted us: He has bestowed upon us ''the light
of the knowledge of the glory of God in the face of Jesus Christ,''
and it is ours to reflect the light, to impart the knowledge, to
manifest the glory, to point to the Saviour's face, and to proclaim
the name of Jesus Christ our Lord. Having such a work before
us, we faint not, but press onward with our whole heart.

I. With no other preface than this we shall ask your attention
this morning, first, to THE SUBJECT OF THAT KNOWLEDGE in
which Paul delighted so much. What was this knowledge which
to his mind was the chief of all, and the most worthy to be
spread? It was the knowledge *of God*. Truly a most needful
and proper knowledge for all God's creatures. For a man not
to know his Maker and Ruler is deplorable ignorance indeed.
The proper study of mankind is God. Paul not only knew
that there is a God, for he had known that before his conversion:
none can more surely believe in the Godhead than did Paul
as a Jew. Nor does he merely intend that he had learned somewhat of the character of God, for that also he had known from
the Old Testament Scriptures before he was met with on the
way to Damascus; but now he had come to know God in a
closer, clearer, and surer way, for he had seen Him incarnate
in the person of the Lord Jesus Christ.

The apostle had also received the knowledge of *"the glory of
God."* Never had the God of Abraham appeared so glorious
as now. God in Christ Jesus had won the adoring wonder of
the apostle's instructed mind. He had known Jehovah's glory
as the One and only God, he had seen that glory in creation
declared by the heavens and displayed upon the earth, he had

beheld that glory in the law which blazed from Sinai and shed its insufferable light upon the face of Moses; but now, beyond all else, he had come to perceive *the glory of God in the face, or person, of Jesus Christ,* and this had won his soul. This special knowledge had been communicated to him at his conversion when Jesus spake to him out of heaven. In this knowledge he had made great advances by experience and by new revelations; but he had not yet learned it to the full, for he was still seeking to know it perfectly by the teaching of the divine Spirit, and we find him saying, "That I may know him, and the power of his resurrection, and the fellowship of his sufferings, being made conformable unto his death."

Paul knew not merely God, but God in Christ Jesus; not merely "the glory of God," but "the glory of God in the face of Jesus Christ." The knowledge dealt with God, but it was Christward knowledge. He pined not for a Christless Theism, but for God in Christ. This, beloved, is the one thing which you and I should aim to know. There are parts of the divine glory which will never be seen by us in this life, speculate as we may. Mysticism would fain pry into the unknowable; you and I may leave dreamers and their dreams, ·and follow the clear light which shines from the face of Jesus. What of God it is needful and beneficial for us to know He has revealed in Christ, and whatsoever is not there, we may rest assured it is unfit and unnecessary for us to know. Truly the revelation is by no means scant, for there is vastly more revealed in the person of Christ than we shall be likely to learn in this mortal life, and even eternity will not be too long for the discovery of all the glory of God which shines forth in the person of the Word made flesh. Those who would supplement Christianity had better first add to the brilliance of the sun or the fulness of the sea. As for us, we are more than satisfied with the revelation of God in the person of our Lord Jesus, and we are persuaded of the truth of His words "he that hath seen me hath seen the Father."

We will for a minute or two consider this glory of God in the face of Jesus Christ *historically.* In every incident of the life of Jesus of Nazareth, the Lord's anointed, there is much of God to be seen. What volumes upon volumes might be written to show God as revealed in every act of Christ from His birth to His death! I see Him as a babe at Bethlehem lying in a manger and there I perceive a choice of glory in the mind of God, for He evidently despises the pomp and glory of the world, which little minds esteem so highly. He might have been born in marble halls, and wrapped in imperial purple, but He scorns these things, and in the manger among the oxen we see a glory which is independent of the trifles of luxury and parade. The glory of God in the person of Jesus asks no aid from the splendour of courts and palaces.

Yet even as a babe He reigns and rules. Mark how the shepherds hasten to salute the new-born King, while the magi from the far-off East bring gold, frankincense, and myrrh, and bow at His feet. When the Lord condescends to show Himself in little things He is still right royal, and commands the homage of mankind. He is as majestic in the minute as in the magnificent, as royal in the babe at Bethlehem as in after days in the Man Who rode through Jerusalem with hosannas. See the holy Child Jesus in the temple when He is but twelve years old, sitting in the midst of the doctors, astonishing them with His questions! What wisdom there was in that Child! Do you not see therein an exhibition of the truth that "the foolishness of God is wiser than men"? Even when God reserves His wisdom, and gives forth utterances fitted for a child, He baffles the wisdom of age and thought. Watch that Youth in the carpenter's shop. See Him planing and sawing, cutting and squaring, working according to His parent's command, till He is thirty years of age.

What learn we here when we see the incarnate God tarrying at the workman's bench? See we not how God can wait? Is not this a masterly display of the leisure of the Eternal? The Infinite is never driven out of His restful pace of conscious strength. Had it been you and I, we should have hastened to begin our life-work long before; we could not have refrained from preaching and teaching for so long a period; but God can wait, and in Christ we see how prudence tempered zeal, and made Him share in that eternal leisure which arises out of confidence that His end is sure. The Godhead was concealed at Bethlehem and Nazareth from the eyes of carnal men; but it is revealed to those who have spiritual sight wherewith to behold the Lord. Even in those early days of our Lord, while yet He was preparing for His great mission, we behold the glory of God in His youthful face, and we adore.

As for His public ministry, how clearly the Godhead is there! Behold Him, brethren, while He feeds five thousand with a few loaves and fishes, and you cannot fail to perceive therein the glory of God in the commissariat of the universe; for the Lord God openeth His hand and supplieth the lack of every living thing. See Him cast out devils, and learn the divine power over evil. Hear Him raise the dead, and reverence the divine prerogative to kill and to make alive. See Him cure the sick, and think you hear Jehovah say, "I wound, I heal." Hear how He speaks, and infallibly reveals the truth, and you will perceive the God of knowledge to Whom the wise-hearted owe their instruction. Set over against each other these two sentences,—"Behold, God exalteth by his power; who teacheth like him?" and "Never man spake like this man."

It is ever the Lord's way to make His truth known to those of humble and truthful hearts, and so did Jesus teach the sincere and lowly among men. Observe how Jesus dwelt among men, wearing the common smock-frock of the peasant, entering their cottages, and sharing their poverty. Mark how He even washed His disciples' feet. Herein we see the condescension of God, Who must stoop to view the skies, and bow to see what angels do, and yet does not disdain to visit the sons of men. In wondrous grace He thinks of us, and has pity upon our low estate. See, too, the Christ of God, my brethren, bearing every day with the taunts of the ungodly, enduring "such contradiction of sinners against himself," and you have a fair picture of the infinite patience and the marvellous longsuffering of God, and this is no small part of His glory.

Note well how Jesus loved His own which were in the world, yea, loved them to the end, and with what tenderness and gentleness He bore with them, as a nurse with her child, for here you see the tenderness and gentleness of God, and the love of the great Father towards His erring children. You read of Jesus receiving sinners and eating with them, and what is this but the Lord God, merciful and gracious, passing by transgression, iniquity, and sin? You see Jesus living as a physician among those diseased by sin, with the one aim of healing their sicknesses; and here you see the pardoning mercy of our God, His delight in salvation, and the joy which He has in mercy. Throughout His ministry, which was mainly a period of humiliation, there gleams forth in the character, acts, and person of Jesus the glory of the everlasting Father. His acts compel us not only to admire but to adore; He is not merely a man whom God favours, He is God Himself.

What shall I say of His death? Oh never did the love of God reveal itself so clearly as when He laid down His life for His sheep, nor did the justice of God ever flame forth so conspicuously as when He would suffer in Himself the curse for sin rather than sin should go unpunished, and the law should be dishonoured. Every attribute of God was focussed at the cross, and he that hath eyes to look through his tears, and see the wounds of Jesus, shall behold more of God there than a whole eternity of providence or an infinity of creation shall ever be able to reveal to him. Well might the trembling centurion, as he watched the cross, exclaim, "Truly this was the Son of God."

Shall I need to remind you, too, of the glory of God in the person of Christ Jesus in His resurrection, when He spoiled principalities and powers, led death captive, and rifled the tomb? That is indeed a godlike speech, "I am he that liveth and was dead, and behold I am alive for evermore, and have the keys of hell and of death." His power, His immortality, His eternal majesty, all shone forth as He left the shades of death.

I will not linger over His ascension when He returned to His own again. Then His Godhead was conspicuous, for He again put on the glory which He had with the Father or ever the world was. Then amid the acclamations of angels and redeemed spirits the glory of the conquering Lord was seen. By His descent He had destroyed the powers of darkness, and then He ascended that He might fill all things as only God can do.

I would only hint at His session at the right hand of God, for there you know how—

> "Adoring saints around Him stand,
> And thrones and powers before Him fall;
> The God shines gracious through the Man,
> And sheds sweet glories on them all."

In heaven they never conceive of Jesus apart from the divine glory which perpetually surrounds Him. No one in heaven doubts His deity, for all fall prostrate before Him, or anon, all seize their harps and wake their strings to the praise of God and the Lamb.

The glory of God will most abundantly be seen in the second advent of our Lord. Whatever of splendour we may expect at the advent, whatever of glory shall surround that reign of a thousand years, or the end when He shall deliver up the kingdom to God, even the Father, in every transaction which prophecy leads us to expect, God in Christ Jesus will be conspicuous, and angelic eyes shall look on with adoring admiration as they see the eternal Father glorious in the person of His Son.

In the person of Jesus we see the glory of God *in the veiling of His splendour*. The Lord is not eager to display Himself: "Verily thou art a God that hidest thyself," said the prophet of old. The world seems to be created rather to hide God than to manifest Him: at least, it is certain that even in the grandest displays of His power we may say with Job, "There was the hiding of his power." Though His light is brightness itself, yet it is only the robe which conceals Him. "Who coverest thyself with light as with a garment." If thus God's glory is seen in the field of creation as a light veiled and shaded to suit

the human eye, we certainly see the life in the face of Jesus
Christ where everything is mild and gentle—full of grace as
well as truth. How softly breaks the divine glory through the
human life of Jesus: a babe in grace may gaze upon this brightness without fear. When Moses' face shone the people could
not look thereon; but when Jesus came from His transfiguration
the people ran to Him and saluted Him. Everything is attractive
in God in Christ Jesus. In Him we see God to the full, but
the Deity so mildly beams through the medium of human flesh
that mortal man may draw near, and look, and live. This glory
in the face of Jesus Christ is assuredly the glory of God, even
though veiled; for thus in every other instance doth God in
measure shine forth. In providence and in nature such a thing
as an unveiled God is not to be seen, and the revelation of God
in Christ is after the same divine manner.

In our Lord Jesus we see the glory of God *in the wondrous
blending of the attributes.* Behold His mercy, for He dies for sinners;
but see His justice, for He sits as judge of quick and dead.
Observe His immutability, for He is the same yesterday, to-day,
and for ever; and see His power, for His voice shakes not only
earth but also heaven. See how infinite is His love, for He
espouses His chosen; but how terrible His wrath, for He consumes His adversaries. All the attributes of Deity are in Him:
power that can lull the tempest, and tenderness that can embrace
little children. The character of Christ is a wonderful com-
bination of all perfections making up one perfection; and so
we see the glory of God in the face of Jesus Christ, for this is
God's glory, that in Him nothing is excessive and nothing is
deficient. He is all that is good and great: in Him is light, and
no darkness at all. Say, is it not so seen in Jesus our Lord?

When I think of God I am led to see His glory *in the outgoing
of His great heart;* for He is altogether unselfish and unsparingly
communicative. We may conceive a period when the Eternal
dwelt alone and had not begun to create. He must have been
inconceivably blessed; but He was not content to be enwrapped
within Himself, and to enjoy perfect bliss alone. He began
to create, and probably formed innumerable beings long before
this world came into existence; and He did this that He might
multiply beings capable of happiness. He delighted to indulge
His heart by deeds of beneficence, manifesting the inherent
goodness of His nature. In whatever God is doing He is con-
sulting the happiness of His creatures; being in Himself independent of all, He loves to bless others. He is living—we speak
with awe in His presence—He is living, even He, not unto
Himself, but living in the lives of others, rejoicing in the joy
of His creatures. This is His glory, and is it not to be seen most

evidently in Christ Jesus, who "saved others, himself he could not save"? Do you not see the great unselfish glory of God in Christ Jesus? When did He ever live unto Himself? What single act of His had a selfish purpose? What word ever sought His own honour? In what deed did He consult His own aggrandisement? Neither in life nor in death did Christ live within Himself: He lived for His people, and died for them. See the glory of God in this!

There are two things I have noticed in the glory of God whenever my soul has been saturated with it, and these I have seen in Jesus. I have stood upon a lofty hill and looked abroad upon the landscape, and seen hill, and dale, and wood, and field, and I have felt as if God had gone forth and spread His presence over all. I have felt *the outflow of Deity*. There was not a pleasant tree, nor a silvery stream, nor a cornfield ripening for the harvest, nor mount shaggy with pines, nor heath purple with heather, but seemed aglow with God. Even as the sun pours himself over all things, so does God; and in the hum of an insect as well as in the crash of a thunderbolt we hear a voice saying, "God is here." God has gone forth out of Himself into the creation, and filled all things. Is not this the feeling of the heart in the presence of Christ? When we come near Him He is the all-pervading spirit. In any of the scenes in which Jesus appears He is omnipresent. Who but He is at Bethlehem, or at Nazareth, or at Jerusalem? Who but He is in the world? Is not He to us the everybody, the one only person of His age? I cannot think of Cæsar or Rome, or all the myriads that dwell on the face of the earth as being anything more than small figures in the background of the picture when Jesus is before me. He is to my mind most clearly the fulness, filling all in all; all the accessories of any scene in which He appears are submerged in the flood of glory which flows from His all-subduing presence. Verily the outgoing glory of God was in Christ.

But you must have had another thought when you have felt the glory of God in nature: you must have felt *the indrawing of all things towards God*. You have felt created things rising unto God as steps to His throne. As you have gazed with rapture on the landscape every tree and hill has seemed to drift towards God, to tend towards Him, to return, in fact, to Him from whom it came. Is it not just so in the life of Christ? He seems to be drawing all things to Himself, gathering together all things in one in His own personality. Some of these things will not move, but yet His attraction has fallen on them, while others fly with alacrity to Him, according to His word, "I, if I be lifted up, will draw all men unto me." Thus those observations of the glory of God, which have been suggested to us by nature, are also abundantly verified in Christ, and we are sure that the glory is the same.

I cannot express my own thoughts to you so clearly and vividly as I would, but this I know, if you ever get a vision of the glory of God in nature, and if you then turn your thoughts toward the Lord's Christ, you will see that the same God is in Him as in the visible universe, and that the same glory shines in Him, only more clearly. There is one God, and that one God is gloriously manifested in Christ Jesus. "No man hath seen God at any time; the only Begotten Son, which is in the bosom of the Father, he hath declared him."

Let us now treat this thought of the glory of God in the person of Christ *by way of experience.* Have you ever heard Christ's doctrine in your soul? If so, you have felt it to be divine, for your heart has perceived its moral and spiritual glory, and you have concluded that God is in it of a truth. Has your heart heard the voice of Christ speaking peace and pardon through the blood? If so, you have known Him to be Lord of all. Did you ever see the fulness of His atonement? Then you have felt that God Himself was there reconciling the world unto Himself. You have understood the union of the two titles, "God, our Saviour." Beloved, you have often felt your Lord's presence, and you have been admitted into intimate communion with Him. Then I know that a profound awe has crept over you which has made you fall at His feet, and in the lowliest reverence of your spirit you have owned Him to be Lord and God. But when He has bent over you in love and said, "Fear not"; when He has opened His heart to you and shown you how dear you are to Him, then the rapture you have felt has been so divine that you have, beyond all question, known Him to be God. There are times when the elevating influence of the presence of Christ has put His Godhead beyond the possibility of question, when we have felt that all the truth we ever heard before had no effect upon us compared with the truth that is in Him; that all the spirits in the world were ineffectual to stir us till His Spirit came into contact with our spirit. In this manner His omnipotent, all-subduing, elevating love has proved Him to be none other than "very God of very God."

Thus have we spoken of the supremely precious object of Christian knowledge.

II. Secondly, let us spend a few words in noticing THE NATURE OF THIS KNOWLEDGE. How, and in what respects, do we know the glory of God in the face of Jesus Christ?

Briefly, first. We know it *by faith.* Upon the testimony of the infallible word we believe and are sure that God is in Christ

Jesus. The Lord hath spoken and said, "This is my beloved Son, hear ye him." We accept as a settled fact the Godhead of the Lord Jesus, and our soul never permits a question upon it. "We know that the Son of God is come, and hath given us an understanding, that we may know him that is true, and we are in him that is true, even in his Son Jesus Christ. This is the true God, and eternal life."

Knowing our Lord's divinity by faith, we next have used our perceptive faculty, and *by consideration and meditation we perceive* that His life furnishes abundant evidence that He was God, for God's glory shines in that life. The more carefully we pay attention to the details given us by the four evangelists, the more is our understanding persuaded that no mere man stands before us. If, my brethren, your spiritual nature was set this task, to try and describe how God would act if He were here, what God would be if He became incarnate and dwelt among men—I am sure you would not have been able to imagine the life of Christ; but if some one had brought to you the description given by the evangelists you would have said, "My task is done: this is indeed a noble conception of God manifest in the flesh." I do not say that the wise men of this world would suppose God to have thus behaved, for their suppositions are sure to be the reverse of the simple, unaffected, open-hearted conduct of Jesus: but this I say, that the pure in heart will at once see that the acts of Christ are like the doings of God. He hath done exactly what a pure intelligence might suppose God would have done. The more we have studied the more we have seen the glory of God in Christ.

And now we have come rather further than this, for we feel an *inward consciousness* that the Deity is in Christ Jesus. It is not merely that we have believed it, and that we somewhat perceive it by observation, but we have come into contact with Christ, and have known therefore that He is God. We love Him, and we also love God, and we perceive that these two are one; and the more we love truth and holiness, and love, which are great traits in the character of God, the more we see of these in Christ Jesus. It is by the heart that we know God and Christ, and as our affections are purified we become sensible of God's presence in Christ. Ofttimes when our soul is in rapt fellowship with Jesus we laugh to scorn the very thought that our Beloved can be less than divine.

Moreover, there is one other thing that hath happened to us while we have been looking at our Lord. Blessed be His name, we begin to grow like Him. Our beholding Him has purified the eye which has gazed on His purity: His brightness has helped our eyesight so that we see much already, and shall

yet see more. The light of the sun blinds us, but the light of
Jesus Christ strengthens the eye. We expect that as we grow
in grace we shall behold more and more of God's glory; but
we shall see it best in the Well-beloved, even in Christ Jesus
our Lord. What a sight of God we shall enjoy in heaven! We
are tending that way, and, as we get nearer and nearer, our
sight and vision of the glory of God in Christ is every day
increased. We know it, then; we know it: we believe it, we
are conscious of it, we are affected by it, we are transformed
by it; and thus at this day we have "the light of the knowledge
of the glory of God in the face of Jesus Christ."

III. Thirdly, let us gratefully review THE MEANS OF THIS
KNOWLEDGE. How have we come at it? That brings us to read
the text again:—"For God, who commanded the light to shine
out of darkness, hath shined in our hearts, to give the light
of the knowledge of the glory of God in the face of Jesus Christ."
Why did not everybody see the glory of God in Jesus Christ
when He was here? It was conspicuous enough. Answer: it
mattereth not how brightly the sun shineth among blind men.
Now, the human heart is blind, it refuses to see God in creation
except after a dim fashion, but it utterly refuses to discern God
in Christ, and therefore He is the despised and rejected of men.
Moreover, there is a god of this world, the prince of darkness,
and since he hates the light he deepens and confirms the natural
darkness of the human mind, lest the light should reach the
heart. He blinds men's minds with error and falsehood and
foul imaginations, blocking up the windows of the soul either
with unclean desires, or with dense ignorance, or with pride.
The reason why we did not at one time perceive the glory of
God in Christ was because we were blind by nature, and were
darkened by the evil one. As only the pure in heart can see
God, we, being impure in heart, could not see God in Christ.
What, then, hath happened to us? To eternal grace be endless
praise, God Himself hath shined into our hearts: that same
God Who said "Light be," and light was, hath shined into our
hearts. You know creation's story, how all things lay in black
darkness. God might have gone on to make a world in darkness if He had pleased, but if He had done so it would have
been to us as though it had never been, for we could not have
perceived it; therefore He early said, "Let there be light."

Now, God's glory in the face of Jesus Christ might have been
all there, and we should never have discerned it, and as far
as we are concerned it would have been as though it had never
been, if the Lord had not entered into us amid the thick darkness and said, "Let there be light." Then burst in the everlasting
morning, the light shined in the darkness, and the darkness

fled before it. Do you recollect the incoming of that illumination? If you do, then I know the first sight you saw by the new light was the glory of God in Jesus Christ: in fact, that light had come on purpose that you might see it; and at this present moment that is the main delight of your soul, the choice subject of your thoughts. In the light of God you have seen the light of the glory of God, as it is written, "In thy light we shall see light."

One thing I want to say to comfort all who believe. Beloved, do you see the glory of God in Christ Jesus? Then let that sight be an evidence to you of your salvation. When our Lord asked His disciples, "Whom do men say that I the Son of man am?" Simon Peter answered, "Thou art the Christ, the Son of the living God." Now, note the reply of the Lord Jesus to that confession: "Blessed art thou, Simon Bar-jona; for flesh and blood hath not revealed it unto you, but my Father which is in heaven." If thou canst delight in God in Christ Jesus, then remember, "no man can say that Jesus is the Christ but by the Holy Ghost," and thou hast said it, and this morning thou art saying it, and therefore the Holy Ghost has come upon thee. "Whosoever believeth that Jesus is the Christ is born of God." Thou believest this, and therefore thou art born of the Father. "Whosoever denieth the Son, the same hath not the Father: but he that acknowledgeth the Son hath the Father also." Thou lovest God, and thou art His: the Spirit of God hath opened thine eyes and thou art saved.

Oh, beloved, do you delight in Jesus Christ? Is He all your salvation, and all your desire? Do you adore Him, do you consecrate yourself to His honour, do you wish to live for Him, and to die for Him? Then be sure that you belong to Him, for it is the mark of the children of God that they love God in Christ Jesus.

IV. So I finish by mentioning, in the fourth place, THE RESPONSIBILITIES OF THIS KNOWLEDGE. There have been considerable debates among the interpreters as to the precise bearing of this text, and some of them think it means that Paul is giving a reason why he preached the gospel. This makes the verse run thus:—"For God, who commanded the light to shine out of darkness, hath shined in our hearts, that we might give out again the light of the knowledge of the glory of God in the face of Jesus Christ." God gave light to the apostles that they might show forth the light of the knowledge of God in the face of Jesus Christ to the nations. I do not know whether this is the exact run of the text, but I know it is true anyhow.

Never is a gleam of light given to any man to hide away, and to spiritual men the great object of their lives, after they have received light, is to reflect that light in all its purity. You must not hoard up the light within yourself; it will not be light to you if you do. Only think of a person when his room is full of sunlight saying to his servant, "Quick, now! Close the shutters, and let us keep this precious light to ourselves." Your room will be in the dark, my friend. So, when a child of God gets the light from Christ's face he must not say "I shall keep this to myself," for that very desire would shut it out. No, let the light shine through you; let it shine everywhere. You have the light that you may reflect it. An object which absorbs light is dark, and we call it black; but hang up a reflector in its place when the sun in shining, and it will not appear black, it will be so bright that you will hardly bear to look at it. An object is itself bright in proportion as it sends back the light which it receives. So you shall find, as a Christian, that, if you absorb light into yourself, you will be black, but if you scatter it abroad you yourself shall be brilliant: you shall be changed into the very image of the light which you have received, you shall become a second sun.

I noticed last Sabbath evening, when I came into this pulpit, that, at the angle of the building before me, on the left hand the sun seemed to be setting, and I saw the brightness of his round face, and yet I knew it to be the wrong quarter of the heavens for the sun to be setting there. Perhaps you will observe that there is a peculiar window on the other side of the street, and it was reflecting the sun so well that I thought it was the sun himself, and I could hardly bear the light. It was not the sun, it was only a window, and yet the radiance was dazzling; and so a man of God, when he receives the light of Christ, can become so perfect a reflector that to common eyes, at any rate, he is brightness itself. He has become transformed from glory to glory as by the image of the Lord.

Brothers and sisters, if you have learned the truth, manifest it, and make it plain to others. Proclaim *the gospel*, not your own thoughts; for it is Christ that you are to make manifest. Teach, not your own judgments, and conclusions, and opinions, but the glory of God in the face of Jesus Christ. Let Jesus manifest Himself in His own light; do not cast a light on Him, or attempt to show the sun with a candle. Do not aim at converting men to your views, but let the light shine for itself and work its own way. Do not colour it by being like a painted window to it, but let the clear white light shine through you that others may behold your Lord.

Scatter your light in all unselfishness. Wish to shine, not that others may say "How bright he is," but that they getting the light may rejoice in the source from which it came to you

and to them. Be willing to make every sacrifice to spread this
light which you have received. Consecrate your entire being
to the making known among the sons of men the glory of Christ.
Oh, I would we had swift messengers to run the world over
to tell the story that God has come down among us. I wish
we had fluent tongues to tell in every language the story that,
coming down among us, God was arrayed in flesh like to our
own: and that He took our sins and carried our sorrows. Oh,
that we had trumpet tongues, to make the message peal through
heaven and earth that God has come among men, and cries,
"Come unto me all ye that labour and are heavy laden, and
I will give you rest."

Oh for a thunder voice, to speak it, or a lightning pen to
write it athwart the heavens, that God hath reconciled the
world unto Himself by the death of His Son, not imputing their
trespasses unto them; and that whosoever believeth in Christ
Jesus hath everlasting life. I cannot command thunder or
lightning, but here are your tongues, go and tell it this afternoon: here is my tongue, and I have tried to tell it, and may
it be silent in the dust of death ere it ceases to declare that one
blessed message, that God in Christ Jesus receives the sons
of men in boundless love. Tell it, brother, with broken accents,
if thou canst not speak it more powerfully. Whisper it, sister,
gently whisper, if to none other yet to thy little children, and
make the name of "Emmanuel, God with us," to be sweet
in thine infant's ears.

Thou art growing in strength and talent, young man, come,
consecrate thyself to this. And thou, grey-beard, ere thou dost
lie down on thy last bed to breathe out thy spirit, tell the love
of Jesus to thy sons that they may tell it to their sons, and hand
it down to coming generations, that mankind may never forget
that the "word was made flesh and dwelt among us, and we
beheld his glory, the glory as of the only begotten of the Father
full of grace and truth." God bless you. Amen.